How to Design & B[uild Patios]

Created and Designed by the Editorial Staff of Ortho Books

Project Editors
Robert J. Beckstrom
Sally W. Smith

Writer
Sharon Ross

Illustrator
Pamela Drury-Wattenmaker

Ortho Books

Publisher
Robert B. Loperena

Editorial Director
Christine Jordan

Manufacturing Director
Ernie S. Tasaki

Managing Editor
Sally W. Smith

Editors
Robert J. Beckstrom
Michael D. Smith

Prepress Supervisor
Linda M. Bouchard

Sales & Marketing Manager
David C. Jose

Publisher's Assistant
Joni Christiansen

Graphics Coordinator
Sally J. French

Address all inquiries to:
Ortho Books
Box 5006
San Ramon, CA 94583-0906

1 2 3 4 5 6 7 8 9
96 97 98 99 2000 01

ISBN 0-89721-284-3
Library of Congress Catalog Card
Number 95-68609

THE SOLARIS GROUP
2527 Camino Ramon
San Ramon, CA 94583-0906

Editorial Coordinator
Cass Dempsey

Copyeditor
Elizabeth Von Radics

Proofreader
Alicia K. Eckley

Indexer
Frances Bowles

Separations by
Color Tech Corp.

Lithographed in the USA by
Banta Book Group

Special Thanks to
Del and Gene Blizzard
Eva and John Breyer
Deborah Cowder
Loretta and Robert Curci
Designer Showcase of the
    Benefit Guild of the East Bay
Margaret and Walt Eden
The San Francisco Decorator
    Showcase
Mr. and Mrs. Paul Schweibinz
Union Street Inn
David Van Ness
Sue Waggener and Steve
    McCraken

Designers & Builders
The names of designers and builders are followed by the page numbers on which their work appears.

Artistic Lighting of San
    Raphael: 25B
Berrington Assoc.: 46
Blue Sky Designs: 26–27
Cynthia Brian, ASID, Starstyle
    Designs: 8
Kevin Campbell: Front
    cover, 6
Jeff Doney/Nick Mein: 1, 11,
    17T, back cover TL
Environmental Creations: 36
Dan Fix Landscape
    Construction: 58–59
Greg Grisamore and
    Assoc.: 15T
Carolyn A. Guy, Barbara
    Argabright, and Peter
    Tourtelotte: 24T and back
    cover BL
John Herbst, Jr., and Assoc.: 85
Katzmaier Newell Kehr: 4–5
The Maccrone Design
    Group: 23
Magrane/Latker Landscape
    Design: 22T
Kate and Dick Maxey: 52,
    back cover TR
Mehus Construction Co.: 53

Jan Moyer Lighting Design:
    3T, 9T
Rogers Gardens: 4–5, back
    cover BR
Jeff Stone, Landscape
    Architect: 14, 16, 19, 22B, 55T
Lynn Winterbotham: 53
Robert Zinkahn: 9B

Photographers
The names of photographers are followed by the page numbers on which their work appears.

Russell Abraham
    Photography: 9B, 21, 53
William Aplin: 47B, 48L
Dennis Bettencourt: 47T
Laurie Black: 49
Dick Christman: 3B, 44–45
Josephine Coatsworth: 20T
Crandall & Crandall: Front
    cover, 4–5, 6, 15T, 18, 26–27,
    36, 46, 48R, 52, 85, back
    cover TR and BR
Julius Fava: 64
David Goldberg: 90, 91
Saxon Holt: 12, 43
Jerry Howard/Positive
    Images: 15B
Susan Lammers: 17B
Michael Landis: 7T, 13, 20B,
    33, 40, 56
Michael McKinley: 7B, 24B,
    25B, 38, 55B
James K. McNair: 10T, 10B
Geoff Nilsen: 22T
Ortho Photo Library: 7C
Kenneth Rice: 1, 3T, 8, 9T, 11,
    17T, 23, 24T, 25T, 28, 58–59,
    back cover TL and BL
Carol Simowitz: 29
Jeff Stone: 14, 16, 19, 22B, 55T

Front Cover
Shangri-la in your backyard? Why not? As you will learn from this book, a successful patio is much more than a lawn replaced by paving. What makes this patio so inviting is the effective blend of many simple elements, including the raised brick planters, the built-in barbecue center, and a nice mixture of sun and shade.

Title Page
The word *patio* implies a flat, horizontal surface—an outdoor platform—but think of your patio as a room with a floor, four walls, and a ceiling. As this elegant courtyard shows, the vertical surfaces and overhead areas offer rich opportunities for design.

Page 3
Top: This patio extends the home's indoor spaces, making an outdoor lifestyle all the more inviting.

Bottom: A visit to your local masonry yard will help you in choosing the best materials for your patio.

Back Cover
Top left: This shady haven features sturdy ground covers and fragrant herbs between the flagstones.

Top right: Interlocking pavers create a colorful and durable courtyard patio.

Bottom left: Outdoor living rises to elegance in a fully furnished patio highlighted by a small fountain.

Bottom right: Just outside the living room, this brick patio invites relaxed enjoyment of a sunny day.

How to Design & Build Patios

PATIOS ARE FOR LIVING

Your home plays a major role in your family's health and happiness by providing a refuge from a stressful world. It can also serve another function that is essential to a sense of well-being: contact with nature. One way to meet both needs at the same time is with a well-designed patio, a simple landscape feature that erases the boundaries between indoors and outdoors, linking your home to your garden with an enchanting and intimate outdoor living space. This book introduces you to that enchantment.

In this chapter you will learn effective ways for enhancing a patio's natural setting while at the same time creating the comforts, privacy, and conveniences of an indoor room. Your patio can become a perfect place for personal leisure and relaxation, recreation and hobbies, entertainment and games. In later chapters you will learn how to draw up a comprehensive plan, select paving materials, and build the patio.

Lush landscaping, fresh air, a sweeping view, and a spot of sun among the trees give this patio an irresistible ambience unmatched by any room in the house.

SUCCESSFUL PATIO DESIGN

A patio is a room. Although outdoors, it has a floor (the paving), walls (the plants, fences, and other features around the edge), and a ceiling (anything from a trellis to the open sky). To design an effective patio, use the same principles as those used for planning indoor rooms.

The Concepts Behind Patio Design

Millions of suburban tract homes suggest that the casual method of patio design seldom works well. Made with an 8 by 10 concrete slab poured in front of sliding glass doors, such a patio is usually too small, uncomfortable, and unattractive to add much pleasure to a family's lifestyle. More important, it does nothing to integrate a house with its property. Yet, it is this ability to unify house and garden that gives a patio its potential for being an intimate, exciting, and enchanting place. Turning that potential into reality requires careful planning and thoughtful design. Both planning and design begin with an understanding that certain features are required for a successful patio, no matter what its size or style.

Essential Features of a Successful Patio

At the beginning stages of design, don't concern yourself with patio size, shape, features, or style, or with the size, shape, or irregularities of your lot. Instead, learn the five "musts" essential to a successful patio: easy access, versatile function, sheltered environment, minimal upkeep, and architectural integrity. Good patio design is a classic example of form following function. It evolves from meeting these basic needs.

• Easy access. Convenience is the key to frequent use. You must be able to walk directly onto a patio, or on a path that leads to it in a logical way, from the indoor room out of which its activity flows. That is the family room in most homes, but there are other options as well, depending upon a family's lifestyle. A master

A key element to the success of this patio is the spacious doorway. Even when the doors are closed, they visually extend and enlarge the indoor space. When open, they encourage movement without creating a bottleneck.

bedroom, for example, can open onto a private patio. Wherever the patio is located, its uses usually involve eating—so it needs to be convenient to the kitchen too.

•Versatility. A successful patio accommodates the activities of everyone in the family. You may want a place to sit and relax and enjoy your garden, but your children probably want a place to play. Although lot size and budget govern what you eventually build, keep everyone's activities in mind as you plan. Then the entire family can and will enjoy the space.

•Sheltered environment. A comfortable patio creates a sense of enclosure without being confining. This intimacy is achieved by building the patio so it provides shelter from the sun, wind, and rain, and screens the area for privacy. Finally, it must be a safe place to relax and play. Safety requires that you choose materials for more than their appearance. Does a material become slippery when wet? Does it have a rough surface that can cause a person to trip? Does it have sharp edges that can cut children's hands and knees? Also plan to provide safety features, such as lights along steps and pathways, and a fence with a lockable gate around a swimming pool.

•Minimal upkeep. No patio is comfortable or pleasurable if it requires constant maintenance and repair. It should be built with durable materials that withstand the ravages of weather, and it should be designed so its surface and the plantings around

Top: Furnishings are grouped on this patio for a wide variety of activities. Center: A wall, an overhead structure, and well-developed plants give this poolside patio a sense of intimacy and enclosure. Bottom: Durable pavings minimize upkeep and maximize swim time.

it require a minimum of routine maintenance, such as sweeping, removing moss, or sealing a porous surface.

•Architectural integrity. The style of an effective patio complements the interior style and exterior architecture of the home, and blends into the garden so it creates a strong visual link between the two.

If a patio doesn't meet these needs, it becomes, at best, an uncomfortable place people use only when absolutely necessary. That is why it is important to evaluate every patio plan, including your own ideas, in terms of how well it meets these basic needs.

Principles of Effective Design

In addition to meeting basic needs, a patio is a harmonious sum of simple parts—paved surface, house walls, garden walls, privacy and wind screens, steps, paths, edging, and planting beds. Combine these elements using the principles of effective design, and you create a handsome patio. These principles are unity, proportion and scale, and contrast.

•Unity. A patio works from inside out so that the house is integrated with its surroundings. This doesn't mean that the patio's details—colors, shapes, textures, and patterns—have to be exactly the same as those inside the home or on its exterior. Rather, it means that a thread of continuity runs through them so the patio's general style, color, and mood harmonize with those of the home. Your goal is to achieve a pleasing blend of design styles.

•Proportion and scale. Proportion is the ratio in size between the parts of a whole. Scale is the size of objects in relationship to one another and to their surroundings. In other words, dining chairs need to be in proportion to a patio table, and the table and chairs together must be in scale with the patio. Together these design elements create balance. An attractive patio provides that balance when its parts are in proportion to one another and its scale is in proportion to the house and yard. Your goal is to achieve an overall feeling of equilibrium.

•Contrast. Visual interest depends on contrast. It is an essential ingredient in successful patio design. You create contrast by using color and texture to accent important parts of the patio. A smooth, gray concrete slab, for example, is quite dull by itself. Border it with a band of coarse red-orange bricks and it

The brick paving of this patio, along with the boxwood hedge, white furniture, and curving step, suggest formality with a touch of casual elegance—a perfect complement to the traditional architectural style of the home.

becomes interesting and pleasing. Together, the two materials create a classic color combination: gray and rust. In addition, the bricks' coarse texture highlights the smoothness of the concrete, creating an interesting balance of textures. Too many contrasts, however, ruin the effect. The goal in effective design is to use contrast to create one or two focal points on the patio.

Patio Design Ideas

Studying photos of patios gives you an easy, effective, and inexpensive way to learn about patio design and develop your own ideas. That is why this book, especially this

Although these patios are different sizes, shapes, colors, and textures, they both "work" because they harmonize with their surroundings, the sizes are appropriate to the purpose, and the materials and colors provide contrast.

first chapter, contains so many photos of patios. The pictures introduce the various patio styles and illustrate the many ways to finish, plant, and furnish a patio. They also show how some combinations of materials work together more effectively than others. Finally, they show you how a patio's design reflects the climate, terrain, and cultural heritage of its area. As you view the many photos, carefully analyze the elements to which you feel most attracted. Visually break down the designs into their parts and analyze their effectiveness based on the design principles outlined above. This process teaches you how they were put together.

The Four Basic Patio Styles

All patio designs can be described in two ways: They are formal or informal, and at the same time they are traditional or contemporary. These broad classes of design describe a tone or feeling rather than a specific set of elements, which is why a contemporary patio can be as formal in style as a traditional patio, and a traditional patio can be informal in style. It's even possible for a patio to be a combination of these types, if the design is carefully handled. Such flexibility allows you plenty of latitude in establishing your own style.

The Formal Patio

A formal patio has a symmetrical, or balanced, arrangement—a style inherited from the ancient Greeks and Romans. If there is an urn on the right side of the patio, a comparable urn is placed in the corresponding spot on the left. Entrances and exits fall in the center of walls, and the design elements fall on axes between them. The scheme is quite orderly. Formal design tends to consist of straight lines and geometric shapes, including circles and half-circles—each balanced by the same shape on the opposite side of the patio. A popular formal patio layout consists of a paved circle in the center, surrounded on all sides by rectangular, square, and triangular planting beds radiating outward. An alternative style surrounds the paved center with concentric circles of curved planting beds. In extremely formal patio design, the trees, bushes, and shrubs are clipped into stately geometric shapes. This style originated in royal gardens and is difficult to maintain without

These patios, both formal, illustrate the traditional patio style (top) and the contemporary style (bottom).

professional help. Most modern formal patios are loose interpretations of this style, so loose they're actually called "semiformal."

The Informal Patio

An informal patio has a casual, or asymmetrical, layout. If there is a clump of trees on the right side of the patio, the corresponding spot on the left side features something with a different size and volume. The emphasis is on harmony rather than absolute balance. An informal layout usually comprises not only curved and wavy lines and flowing shapes, but straight and geometric lines as well. The paved surface usually meanders across the yard in a flowing, free-form fashion. When it consists of straight lines, they zig and zag so they create an asymmetrical shape. Whatever the shape of the pavement of an informal patio, its plantings are massed so they flow casually around the paved surface. The clumps of flowers, and the trees and shrubs that accompany them, grow in their natural shapes. This makes the informal patio the easiest to maintain.

The Traditional Patio

One word describes the feeling of a traditional patio: *warm.* This familiar, comfortable, and secure style has evolved from English origins, which is why you probably think of New England—or even of England itself—when you see this patio style. Traditional patios with formal or semiformal layouts have many

Rather than replace this broken and deteriorating patio, the homeowner planted herbs in the cracks and transformed an eyesore into a pleasant retreat. The casual placement of amenities, asymmetrical design, and clumped plantings give this patio an informal air.

of the decorative details found in Georgian, Federal, and Greek Revival architecture. They evoke the feeling of a courtyard or terrace, and they make liberal use of fountains, benches, columns, balustrades, and urns as decorative motifs. However, a traditional patio also can have an informal style. Country-style patios fall into this classification. The informal traditional patio is just as orderly, but it's built with more casual materials. Steps on a formal traditional patio, for example, are built with uniform materials such as brick, so they have a clean, crisp, well-defined edge. Steps on an informal traditional patio may consist of dry-stacked stones with rough edges. Brick is the favored paving material, with flat native stone running a close second. Both materials are laid in orderly geometric patterns on formal patios, and in random patterns on informal patios. Brick or rubble stones are used for retaining and seating walls. And whether the patio is formal or informal, the emphasis is on lush, full foliage and flowers.

The Contemporary Patio

Cool and serene but comfortable is the best way to describe a contemporary patio. This style is quite architectural. Emphasis is on using simple geometric shapes and long, clean lines to define the space, create contrasting layers of pattern, and forge vistas that direct the eye beyond the patio. Most often, the layout is asymmetrical, with harmony achieved by balancing opposing shapes; however, this style also works in symmetrical arrangements. For example, a set of evenly spaced and perfectly aligned posts can support the front edge of a trellis over a contemporary patio. Sometimes the structural underpinnings show, becoming part of the decorative motif. This contemporary style, called "industrial" or "high tech," evolved from the Bauhaus and International architectural movements. Other times, the patio reflects a Japanese influence. To prevent monotony, there is much more emphasis on color, texture, and light patterns than is found in traditional patios.

All patio styles fall into these basic design categories, but variations in climate, terrain, and historical and ethnic heritage often determine the surface characteristics of patios in different regions of the country.

Major Regional Influences in Patio Design

There's a reason why you find traditional New England–style patios in such unlikely places as Kansas City, Dallas, Los Angeles, and Seattle. English architecture and gardens have been the bellwether of good taste in much of this country since its beginning. The design tide is slowly shifting, however, to an emphasis on using local paving materials and native plants and flowers. The reasons are simple: Indigenous paving materials are cost effective because they don't have to be shipped over long distances; and indigenous plants thrive in the local climate, so they don't require constant maintenance and expensive inputs, especially scarce water. As a result, distinct variations on the four basic patio styles have evolved in different parts of the country (although the traditional patio that originated on the East Coast remains the most popular patio style throughout the United States today).

Contemporary patio style often includes Japanese influences, such as the reflecting pool, manicured garden, and footbridge in this serene setting.

The Eastern Patio

The traditional patio described on page 11 is the quintessential eastern patio—the dominant style from New England to Georgia. It also dominates the South, through New Orleans to Houston. This style evolved from the region's Colonial origins and the English architecture favored by the nation's early wealthy families. By the time you get to New Orleans, it shows French and Spanish influences too. This patio usually abuts the house, which then forms one of its walls. Whether formal, semiformal, or informal in design, the eastern patio has either a brick or a quarried-stone floor. The use of brick reflects the East's Colonial roots. The use of stone is a result of the abundant supply of natural stone available throughout this mountainous region. From limestone and bluestone to granite and marble, any stone that is handsome in color and can be cut into dimensional sizes can be used to floor a patio. These paving materials are laid in orderly, subtle decorative patterns that complement traditional architecture.

The same materials are used to build seating walls along the patio perimeter. These walls often contain planting boxes, so the garden truly spills onto the patio. Beyond these low walls, flower beds, shrubs, and trees create the other walls of the patio. In the North you find few trellises or pergolas, because intense sun is not a problem. Instead, a patio is open to the sky, and a canopy of tree branches provides what shade is needed.

The farther south you go, the more common patio roofs become, because the hot, humid climate demands protection from the sun. These shade structures are usually built of wood, which is painted or left natural. Patios in the South, which are often called terraces, have a more lush or romantic feel because of the longer growing season and greater variety of available plants. Southern patios are also more likely to be built around or adjacent to swimming pools, because year-round outdoor living is possible.

Some of the elements that characterize this patio as eastern style are the brick paving, its location next to the house, lush greenery, and a canopy of tree branches overhead.

13

The Southwestern Patio

A patio has a specific purpose in this arid region of the country: to screen out the desert. If such an effect is not possible, the patio is designed to soften the view of the desert and make this little corner of it habitable. It has another purpose too. Open space is abundant in this region—in the house and in the yard—so patios are designed to break the barrier between the two and maximize the potential for outdoor living. Walls, columns, and arbors define the space and create the feeling of a sheltered courtyard.

This style, reflecting the region's Spanish and Indian heritage, appears in two common versions. One, in which the mission elements dominate, is quite old-world, or traditional. The other is contemporary, with emphasis on simple geometric planes that suggest, rather than re-create, original forms. Either way, patio walls are high and constructed with materials such as poured concrete or concrete block covered with stucco. The patio floor is paved with Mexican pavers, adobe, or divided concrete slabs. Natural sandstone and slate tiles also are popular paving materials. The concrete, whether for paving or for walls, often is pigmented to tone down its grayness and take on the subtle colors of the desert. Sometimes it is even brightly colored. Vivid, patterned ceramic tiles are used to border swimming pools and fountains and provide decorative accents throughout the patio space. And, somewhere on every patio, there is a fountain providing the cooling, soothing ambience created by the sight and sound of falling water.

The Southern California Patio

Although Southern California–style patios often feature southwestern design elements, they have an exuberance all their own. Their designs make lavish use of bold paving materials, dramatic spatial arrangements, and lush plantings. These elements reflect the personal freedom and the physical comfort of the Golden State lifestyle. Here it is possible to truly live outdoors year-round, and it is not uncommon for a patio and its adjacent plantings to take over an entire backyard, lot line to lot line. Most Southern California patios have a swimming pool, which often dominates the space in a small lot. Bold paving materials laid in dramatic patterns reclaim balance in the yard. Often the paving extends over the edge of the swimming pool, creating a natural look. Plants, boulders, and other natural materials placed around the perimeter create a smooth transition between pool and garden. A shade structure is essential over at least part of the patio because of the intense sun.

The Pacific Northwest Patio

This region's patios reflect its close association with Asia, especially Japan. The Pacific Northwest style emphasizes harmonious contrasts in textures, shapes, and colors. To create this look, patios have asymmetrical layouts and are paved with native stone laid in random patterns. Columbia River basalt is a favorite paving material. A dense volcanic rock, it has a rough texture that doesn't get slippery when wet, an important consideration in such a rainy climate. Planting beds filled with boulders, cobbled rocks, gravel, or sand are interspersed among the paved areas. The stones provide a serene backdrop for plants and other objects. Elements selected for their different sizes and volumes are precisely arranged in asymmetrical groupings that form imaginary triangles with unequal sides. This gives the arrangement balance despite its asymmetry. Although these

Although not located in the desert, this patio has a distinctive southwestern feeling because of the earth-colored pavers, boldly colored tile, stucco walls, and fountain.

triangles are formed on both the vertical and the horizontal planes, the horizontal plane dominates, which is why these patios seem so spacious, even when they are quite small. This is also why their walls—consisting of vegetation, wood, or stone—seem to disappear from view. Patio ceilings are usually composed of the open sky or a canopy of tree branches; however, small shelters are often provided for protection against the ever-present rain. Whether authentically Japanese in style, a loose interpretation, or simply based on the design principles embodied in Japanese philosophy, these patios seem more completely integrated into the garden than other types of patios. This is due to their harmonious use of natural materials in their natural state.

This rambling Southern California patio (top), with lounging areas shaded by broad roof overhangs and a swimming pool close at hand, suggests year-round outdoor living. A patio in the Pacific Northwest style (bottom), integrated perfectly into the landscape, emphasizes nature.

15

CREATING THE PATIO LIFESTYLE

A successful patio is much more than a paved surface furnished with some lawn chairs and a grill. It is a total environment created by combining a number of essential elements to achieve visual beauty and personal comfort. Your goal is to provide people with the same intimate atmosphere they find inside your home.

Make a True Outdoor Room

Begin by concentrating on the style and features you want your patio to have. Keep in mind that outdoor rooms have much in common with indoor rooms. In addition to a floor, ceiling, and walls, they have furnishings, other amenities, and mechanical support systems that combine to make them comfortable and livable spaces. Also as with indoor rooms, it's important to give these elements careful consideration so they add to rather than detract from your patio style.

Elements That Define the Space

The hard surfaces of a patio—its pavement, walls, and any overhead structures—define its fundamental space and determine its basic style; and the materials with which you build these structures can consume as much as 75 percent of your budget. The landscape plantings and garden beds that surround the patio also play a powerful role in defining its basic space and establishing its overall style. When considering all of these basic elements, make your choices carefully.

Flooring Options

The abundant choices of paving materials—with all their variations—make the process of choosing one seem quite daunting. However, the myriad possibilities fall into seven basic groups: poured concrete, brick, concrete pavers, stone, tile, adobe, and wood. (For a detailed discussion of these materials, see "Choosing Patio Materials," beginning on page 45.)

Each material has unique characteristics that give it a mood or tone that sets the patio style. To make the selection task easier, think of the paving as a unifying element,

Paving a formal patio with an informal material, such as flagstone, is a risky practice, but here the risk paid off with rich textures and warm colors. The stone's even joints and crisp edges prevent the joint lines from competing with the layout axis.

a low-key but stylish floor covering for your patio. Choose carefully to get the mood you desire. If your choice isn't suitable for building walls, select a wall material that complements or coordinates with it.

Structural Walls

A structural wall defines the patio border and creates a sense of enclosure, but in a rigid way. When a patio is adjacent to a house, one or more of the home's exterior walls automatically become patio walls too, which may be all the enclosure a patio needs. Certainly, it is all the high-wall enclosure most patios require. A patio may also need low walls to provide supplementary seating, control a slope, retain a steep hillside, or serve as a divider between

Top: A lattice screen is an excellent device to keep tall walls from closing in on a patio. Bottom: An intriguing pavement of wood blocks and dividers enhances the natural setting of this patio.

17

The roof of this shade structure is stepped up at the outer level to let in more sunlight during winter months and to open up the view.

patio areas. Seating walls that double as planters are especially popular on traditional-style patios. Such walls influence the patio design, and the materials they are built with must harmonize with the paving material.

High walls provide complete enclosure and privacy, but they also block view and ventilation. Unless you are trying to create a small and intensely intimate patio space, they belong on the outer perimeter of the lot. High walls require concrete footings and mortar joints for stability. As you study walls, consider how they will look in relationship to the patio, the house, and the yard.

Patio Roofs

Most patios need some protection from the sun. A simple roof structure such as a trellis or pergola provides shade in an attractive and inexpensive way. These roof structures are made with a basic post-and-beam frame topped with a screening material, usually evenly spaced rafters. Any number of materials can be used to make the frame, from pressure-treated lumber or steel posts to concrete or stucco columns. The same is true for the screening material, the most common and successful of which include lath, batten, latticework, woven wood materials, and lumber. Lumber rafters give you the most stable, permanent, and architecturally pleasing patio shelter.

Whatever structural elements you use, their shape, texture, and color must harmonize with those of the patio, house, and garden. A patio roof may be freestanding or attached to the house, but it must be constructed in such a way that it admits sunlight at comfortable times of the day and effectively shades the patio when the sun is high and intense.

Windbreaks and Privacy Screens

To be truly comfortable, a patio must be sheltered from the neighbors' view as well as from the elements. Ideally, this protection is provided by vegetation. Strategically placed hedges and trees will shelter the patio from wind and noise and provide shade and privacy while maintaining a natural link between the patio and garden.

When foliage is not an option, a vertical screen is the next best choice. A permanent screen is more effective than a wall because it protects the patio while preserving an open, airy feel. Such a screen can be made from a number of materials. A roll-down shade of woven wood or fabric, for example, is a workable choice where such protection is necessary only occasionally—it can be lowered and raised as needed, so it is largely unobtrusive.

A freestanding wood screen, on the other hand, gives a stable, permanent feel and adds an attractive decorative element to a patio. It protects without constricting the space or blocking ventilation.

It can also be used to conceal such unsightly necessities as air conditioners, utility meters, trash cans, and pool pumps. However, like a patio roof, a wood screen makes a strong visual statement, so it must be designed to harmonize with the patio, house, and garden. Structurally, a freestanding screen is fairly simple to build. It consists of a wood frame filled with latticework or diagonal slats of lath, batten, or lumber. The closer together the slats, the more solid the screen and the more protection it provides.

Landscaping and Garden Beds

Most patio walls are illusory. Rather than physical walls that enclose the entire space (with the exception of any house walls adjacent to the patio), they are visual perceptions. They consist primarily of landscape plantings and garden beds that surround the patio, giving it spatial definition and a sense of enclosure. Such perceived containment is appropriate because the design focuses on the patio itself. Some patios, however, are oriented outward to a

This low stucco wall with a lattice screen harmonizes beautifully with the patio materials to create privacy, provide a windbreak, and add visual interest.

spectacular view. In such fortunate situations, the spatial framework of the patio is arranged to focus attention outward.

Where these illusory walls go and what they look like greatly influence patio style. They also determine how much upkeep the patio will require. The landscape and garden elements of a patio need not be elaborate to be effective. A simple paved surface that gives over to lawn, with flower beds and shrubs placed along the border of the lot, works especially well in small yards. An equally effective plan is surrounding a small yard with a wall or fence bordered with plants, and then filling the yard, up to the planting beds, with patio surface. Another simple, low-upkeep layout consists of low

Both of these patios include diverse landscaping elements that shape and enclose the patio, break up large areas, and provide opportunities for people to interact with nature.

hedges or ground-level flower beds bordering the edges of a patio. Placing an outcropping of small boulders in such a flat flower bed provides visual relief; planting a tree has the same effect, plus it provides shade. Raised beds or planter boxes can be used to extend the architectural lines of the house around part of the patio border. Also, a low but well-planted berm area between the patio and the rest of the yard provides definition and privacy without being obtrusive. Remember, the closer a garden is to a patio, the more intimate and hospitable that patio seems.

If you prefer not to have a lot of flower beds to maintain, bring the garden onto the patio by letting plants climb on trellises, wind screens, and walls, including house walls. Plants in hanging pots and baskets and in containers on the patio surface also bring color and texture to the space.

Additions That Enhance the Space

Structural elements and landscaping plants give the patio its basic style, but there are other items that can add to the enjoyment and usefulness of a patio. Some, such as lighting

The simple appeal of this patio, hardly more than a resting place along a brick path, is the intimate contact it provides with the flowers, plants, and trees surrounding it.

Pools range in style from small accent pools made with decorative liner pans to large, formal reflecting pools made of masonry. In between lie pools that look natural because they include waterfalls and are surrounded by flat stones or small boulders. These can be built with liner kits or with hand-packed concrete shells. To look truly natural, they must have irregular shapes and rounded edges. All require a circulating pump to move and aerate the water, and a filter to keep the water clean. The appeal of a pool may be enhanced by the addition of goldfish or water plants.

Patio fountains range from spill units, which drop water in a single stream into a pool, to spray fountains that shoot water upward in a pattern. There also are splash fountains, which force water up through a piece of sculpture such as a statue or a free-standing fountain.

Although do-it-yourself fountain and pool kits are available at garden-supply centers, complex installations are hard to design, install, and maintain. It is also difficult to make them look natural. If you want anything more than a rudimentary pool or fountain for your patio, have it designed and installed by a landscape professional.

Swimming Pools and Spas

Few backyard amenities could be more enticing than a patio with a swimming pool or spa, but including one in a patio design involves a wide range of logistical problems—major

Top: This swim spa provides a pleasant place to swim and leaves enough space for a small patio. Bottom: Bold colors, the sound of splashing water, and a prominent location make this fountain a major addition to the patio.

or furniture, may seem like incidental finishing touches, but they should be chosen with the same care as the structural elements. Other things, such as a swimming pool, are powerful elements in their own right. When planned carefully, however, they can enhance the appeal and livability of the patio, rather than compete with it.

Garden Pools and Fountains

The musical sound of falling water has a profound effect—it makes people feel cooler and calmer. Water is so aesthetically pleasing, in fact, that pools, waterfalls, and fountains are often incorporated into patios, their size and shape limited only by imagination, space, and budget.

This attractive patio might have been dominated by the swimming pool, but the paving and landscaping around the pool hold their own with a blend of rich textures, contrasting colors, and interesting lines.

site modifications, complex mechanical systems, and confusing legal restrictions that include tough code specifications. These make the installation complicated and expensive. If you want your patio to include a swimming pool, hire a landscape professional to help you with the design and installation.

A spa or hot tub, however, is highly suited to do-it-yourself installation. First, understand the difference between the two. A spa is usually made of molded fiberglass or acrylic. There is a wide variety of free-form shapes and sizes; some units are large enough to hold 16 people at a time. In addition to its jets, a spa includes such features as integral contoured

seats and different water depths. Whatever its shell composition, a spa is rigid but it is not self-supporting, which means it must be installed below grade. First you dig a large hole and pour concrete footings at its base. When the footings are set, put the spa in place and backfill around it with sand. Finally, install decking around the perimeter. The compact mechanical system—water lines, pump, filter, and heater—goes in an above-ground cabinet connected to the spa by underground lines. Terrain and the cost of running the lines determine where the spa and mechanical system can be located.

A hot tub is a large wood tub with straight sides that

stands above ground. A hot tub is much easier to install than a spa, but is heavy when filled with water and requires a strong foundation. It also needs adequate air circulation so the wood doesn't rot, which is why most hot tubs are set on raised decks or platforms with the mechanical systems installed underneath, concealed by deck skirting.

Consider how much space a spa or hot tub consumes and how you can place it convenient to the house without crowding or dominating the patio. You should be able to walk to a spa or hot tub in your bare feet, and it should be sheltered from sun and wind and have a fair degree of privacy. Consider screening

it with a modified gazebo, pergola, or screen wall, and be prepared to meet all local zoning ordinances pertaining to covers, fencing requirements, and setbacks.

Grills

Outdoor cooking, or grilling, is one of the principal pleasures associated with a patio. You can use a portable grill stationed on the patio, a built-in barbecue pit near the back door, or a fairly elaborate outdoor kitchen. Whatever the facility, its immediate surroundings should include preparation and serving space, storage cabinets, and a sit-down eating area. Ideally, both the cooking and eating areas are at least partially sheltered by a trellis, pergola, or gazebo. Consider how water pipes, drainpipes, and electrical lines can be routed from the house. This is not a problem for attached patios, because the lines come through the exterior wall. For detached patios, however, the lines will have to run through the ground and under the paving. All outdoor electrical receptacles, light fixtures, and switches must be protected by weathertight boxes. In addition, each outdoor receptacle must be protected by a ground fault circuit interrupter (GFCI) that shuts off the power if there is a short in the circuit.

Furniture

Finding furniture in the right style for your patio will not be a problem. On the contrary, you will find yourself confronted with a bewildering array of outdoor furniture in

a seemingly infinite number of styles, colors, and materials, ranging from aluminum, wrought iron, steel, and wood to synthetic wicker, reed, rattan, and plastic. The first requirement is to not get too much. Spaciousness is one of the best features of a patio, so don't crowd it with too much furniture. Instead, buy only indispensable pieces, such as tables and chairs that you will use all the time, and arrange them in conversational groupings, just as you would in an indoor room. Make use of built-in benches or seating walls for overflow seating; such built-ins often provide the majority of the seating on patios with limited space.

Top: A visit to a designer showcase or a patio furniture showroom will give you lots of ideas for furnishing your patio. Bottom: Patios are meant for outdoor cooking, whether on a traditional brick barbecue or a gas grill.

For a cohesive look, furniture should have materials or design elements common to the overall style of the patio. In addition to being attractive and comfortable, it must be weather-resistant. If you have to store the furniture during the winter, buy pieces that are easily moveable and that either stack or fold for compact storage.

Lighting

There is something about the intimacy of a patio that says you need light at night—but you don't want it to be too bright, which is why, typically, low-voltage landscape fixtures are used for patio lighting. They operate off a transformer that reduces standard household current from 120 volts to 12 volts. The result is subdued lighting that is safe, energy efficient, and inexpensive. This type of lighting can be achieved from a wide range of fixtures. There are well lights and portable uplights for highlighting foliage; spread lights for lighting paths and for outlining garden beds and patio boundaries; wall washers for illuminating walls; downlights for accenting special features such as statuary; and strings of minilights for lighting steps and balustrades. These fixtures also come in a variety of shapes, from utilitarian to sculptural. They are most often made of wood (redwood, cedar, or teak), plastic, or cast or extruded aluminum. More expensive, decorative fixtures are made of bronze, copper, or stone.

A patio should also have some standard 120-volt light-ing, because it produces bright light that can be projected over a wide area. Also, 120-volt receptacles accept plugs for power tools, patio heaters, and other electrical appliances. This full lighting is particularly necessary by the door into the house and in the cooking and eating area. Such standard lighting serves as backup and emergency lights for other areas as well.

Lighting experts recommend that you first choose the bulb and the lighting effect you want, then select a shielded fixture appropriate to the bulb and the style of the patio. Such fixtures hide the bulb behind an opaque covering so the light appears as a warm glow rather than as a hot spot.

Planning outdoor lighting requires a fair degree of finesse. Take a sketch of your patio to a lighting showroom and ask the lighting designer to help you plan its lighting scheme. The service is usually free of charge if you buy your fixtures from that company.

Top: The fixture on the left is 120-volt and requires standard house wiring. The low-voltage fixtures on the right require a transformer, but the wiring is quite simple to install. Bottom: Avoid harsh floodlights for patio lighting. Diffused area lights and a few accent lights should provide enough illumination; if not, light a few candles.

DESIGNING YOUR PATIO

*Although the term **design** implies artistic inspiration and a flair for the dramatic, most of the design process involves focusing on a host of practical details that you have been able to ignore until now—details such as the intended uses of the patio, the size of the lot, its shape and terrain, and its orientation to the sun. You need to understand these elements because they influence the location, size, and shape of your patio. Indirectly, they also influence your patio's style and features. By focusing on the details, you will find that a successful patio design emerges almost on its own.*

The first part of this chapter guides you in planning the location, size, shape, and style of your patio. The second part shows you how to put your ideas on paper and work toward developing a site plan.

You can almost re-create the design process yourself for this smart and attractive patio by studying the details and asking the same questions the owners had to ask. How large? What shape? Where to sit? Where can we entertain? Which direction has the best views? Do we need shade? Is the kitchen handy? How can we enclose the space? What materials and colors should we use? What kind of plants do we want? How will it look from inside the house?

CHOOSING A LOCATION, SIZE & SHAPE

Think of your patio as an addition to your home. Where would you put an indoor room that you expected to perform the same functions you expect of your patio? You will gain clear insight into the best location for your patio by concentrating on how it should serve your home.

Determining Your Family's Needs

Copying someone else's ideas without evaluating them in terms of the family's specific needs is one of the biggest mistakes people make when designing a patio. A patio is successful only if it fits the way you and your family actually live. The first step is to gather everyone together, including small children, and talk about how you live and what you want the patio to do for each of you individually and as a family. Use this opportunity to generate a wish list; this is fantasy time, so don't hold back. Such free discussion—without considering practical limitations and restrictions—reveals what people really want. Making a wish list is easiest if you put each idea in a function category. Typically, people ask that a patio provide a place for five basic functions: personal relaxation, entertainment, children's play, recreation, and gardening.

•Personal relaxation. This is the universal given. Everyone wants a relaxing place to sit and enjoy the outdoors. A patio needs comfortable seating—both moveable and built-in—in sufficient quantity to accommodate everyone in the family simultaneously if necessary. Does relaxation for your family include dining alfresco? If so, you need adequate table space—and probably a portable or built-in grill as well.

•Entertainment. Many people say they plan to entertain, but they never do. Does this describe your family? If so, be honest with yourselves, and don't add features or space for entertaining that you won't use. However, don't overlook the informal entertaining needs of teenagers (or preteens) in the family. If you do entertain, is it casual or formal? Large groups or small? If you like casual outdoor entertaining, determine what extra features you might require. If

This patio includes a sandbox and children's play area, with storage space for toys located nearby. The boards stacked beside the sandbox are for covering it at night.

you host small groups, you may not need anything beyond what's necessary for meeting your family's needs. But if you entertain large groups, especially frequently, you need sufficient seating, cooking, and dining facilities. And don't overlook the importance of providing adequate lighting at night.

•Children's play. Do you need a play area for small children on or adjacent to a patio? For how many children? How old are they? Is your yard the neighborhood playground? If so, add the neighbor kids to your head count. If the children are about to outgrow one play stage—the sandbox, for example—skip that and instead incorporate elements suitable to the next age group. Swings, climbers, tree forts, and playhouses are popular with children of every age, through the preteens. Should such items be placed on the patio, adjacent to it, or nearby? Do older children need a place to play basketball or other games? Does that have to be done on the patio, or can it be done in the driveway?

•Recreation. Do you want a swimming pool? It involves a lot in terms of maintenance. But if you have older children and teenagers, a pool is an ideal way to keep your kids and their friends at your house, where you can keep an eye on them. If a pool seems like too much, how about a hot tub or spa? These make excellent hubs for family togetherness as well as for entertaining friends.

•Gardening. Here, more than anywhere else in the patio plan, people often take on more than they can or want to handle. A lushly planted yard looks wonderful in a photograph, but it has to be maintained. Be realistic about the type of gardener you are and the time you have to devote to it. If you don't necessarily have a green thumb, don't plan a landscape suitable only to an enthusiast. Even if you love gardening, keep your planting plan simple and geared to low maintenance.

When you have your wish list for each function category, prioritize the desired features as a family. Start with the "musts" and end with those features that are desirable but of lesser importance. Consider practicality, and be flexible: Many ideas can be combined or modified, and others can be accommodated elsewhere in the house or yard.

Use the final list as a guide to designing your patio. Start by assigning the functional areas to different parts of the patio; some of these may overlap. As the design develops, be prepared to make compromises. Space and budgets sometimes necessitate discarding some dreams. By using your prioritized list so you eliminate the least important items, you get a patio that fits your family.

Site Considerations

Typically, a patio is placed adjacent to the house so you can walk directly onto it. That's why you think of a patio as being an addition to

your house—but to what part of the house? The back or side yards are the most common locations. Which is best? Several factors influence this decision. One is the uses you plan for the patio. Others include local legal requirements, the size and shape of the lot, how the home sits on the lot, and its orientation to the sun. Take all these things into consideration when deciding on the patio location.

What You Can Do Legally

Before you do anything else, review local regulations governing patios. There are three types of such rules: building

codes, zoning ordinances, and deed restrictions.

•Building codes. Every community has a building code that governs how a house and everything related to it, including a patio, is built. This code exists to ensure that the house is safe to live in and won't become a hazard or an eyesore. How does your local building code address patio construction? Do any of the requirements affect location, such as a minimum distance from underground utility lines or the need to isolate any connections between a patio and a house foundation?

•Zoning ordinances. A community uses ordinances to regulate how property is used

Simplicity of form—a sweeping curve of colored concrete—allows this patio to fulfill many functions, from a viewing platform to a poolside entertaining area.

and how a building is placed on that property. Such regulations establish minimum setbacks from the property line, minimum and maximum heights for structures, utility easements, and the amount of lot surface that can be covered by structures, which include patios and decks. Lot coverage ordinances have become quite restrictive in recent years in order to control runoff into storm sewers, streams, and lakes. If any ordinance makes it too difficult to build your patio where you need it, you can petition the local planning commission for a variance. With the exception of lot coverage, you probably won't be turned down if you get your neighbors to agree with your request before you apply.

• Deed restrictions. Communities that want to maintain a certain market value or architectural style for their homes often write specific restrictions into the property deeds. Such restraints can govern the types of improvements you can make, the style in which you execute them, the types of materials you can use, and even where you can put specific improvements on your property.

Before you start planning the patio, determine which legal restrictions will apply. There is no point developing a patio design only to discover that your community won't let you build it the way you want or, worse yet, let you build it at all. Once you know what legal requirements you are dealing with, proceed with making your plans.

Analyze Your Yard

Now study the features of your yard. How large is it? What is its shape and contour? Is it basically flat? If so, building a patio won't be complicated. But if the yard lies on a slope or hill, or is heavily graded for drainage, you'll need to excavate a flat area for the patio. In that case, how will you provide for drainage? For retaining the slope or hill? For steps? This simple inventory quickly points out areas of the yard that should not be used for a patio; it also shows you problems that can be corrected by the existence of one.

Look at other features that will affect the patio. Is the yard filled with mature trees, or is it just lawn? Do your neighbors have big trees that border your property? What about foundation plantings, garden beds, fences, walls, walkways, and other features around your home and yard? Is there an attractive view you want to take advantage of? Where are the traffic lanes between the house and different parts of the yard; between your yard and your neighbors' yards? How efficient is the drainage on your lot during a heavy rain? Do you have problems with street traffic and noise? All these factors influence a patio, so consider them carefully as you make your plans.

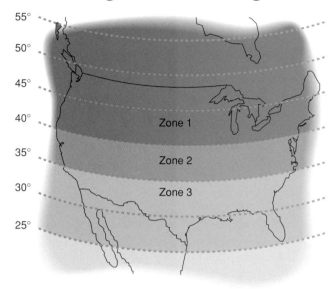

Determining Hours of Sunlight

Start by determining the zone on the map. Then find the position of the sun at noon on the chart below for the daylight hours throughout the year.

	Position of Sun at Noon			Daylight Hours		
	12/21	3/21 & 9/21	6/21	12/21	3/21 & 9/21	6/21
Zone 1	21°	45°	69°	8	12	16
Zone 2	29°	53°	76°	9	12	15
Zone 3	37°	60°	83°	10	12	14

Follow the Sun

Most people view the sun and the patio as two parts of a marvelous whole. They want their outdoor room to be sunny and warm most of the day, but also cool and shady during certain seasons. Begin by learning which direction your house faces. You may already know this, or it may be recorded on your home's plat plan or blueprints; you can also buy an inexpensive compass at a hardware store and take a reading.

Which direction is the logical place for you to attach a patio to your house? In theory, a patio placed on the south side of the house is warm and sunny all day because the sun never leaves it as it moves east to west. A north-side patio is just the opposite; it gets sun exposure only on those sections that extend well beyond the shadow cast by the house. It is probably cool except on the hottest, most humid days. An east-facing patio receives pleasant morning sun and is cool throughout the day; a west-facing patio gets the hot afternoon sun. These patterns are generalizations, however; most sites have their own individual circumstances.

The Sun's Seasonal Changes

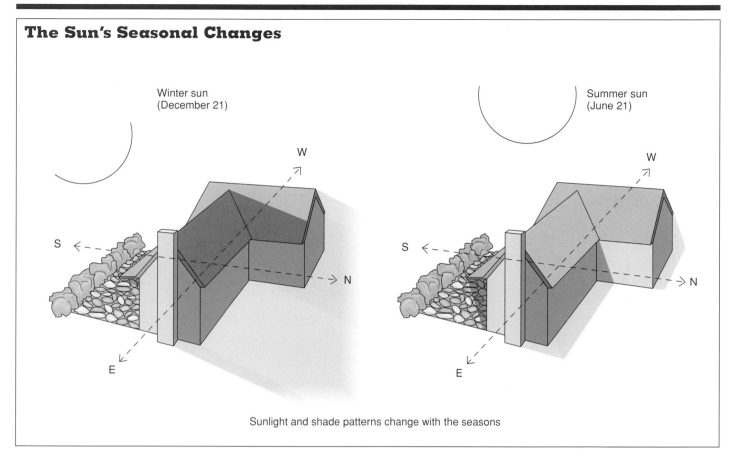

Winter sun
(December 21)

Summer sun
(June 21)

Sunlight and shade patterns change with the seasons

In reality, most houses don't fall on a true north-south or east-west axis, but rather somewhere in between, which means an attached patio probably falls somewhere in between too. This is often advantageous because it combines the sun/shade patterns of two directions. A patio located on the southeast side of a house, for example, gets sun much of the day but escapes the last of the hot afternoon sun.

If placing the patio next to the house where you need it doesn't give you the sun exposure you desire, consider other options. One is to build a patio away from the house but linked to it by a pathway. Another is to build two interrelated patios—one attached to the house and one out in the yard—connected by a pathway.

To find a suitable separate location, spend several summer days studying how the sun and shade patterns fall in your yard and garden. Look for a spot that gets sun most of the day, keeping in mind that some shade is desirable, especially during the late afternoon. Perhaps you'll get lucky and find just such a place that also is reasonably accessible to the house. If such a sunny spot has no shade whatsoever, you can always add a patio roof.

The region and time of year also determine the sun and shade patterns. At midsummer, June 21, the sun is directly overhead and the day is long. By midwinter, December 21, it is low in the sky and the day is short. Short days and low sun angles aren't significant if you live in a northern climate and use your patio only from late spring through the fall. But if you live in a warmer region and use your patio nearly year-round, take these factors into consideration too.

Controlling the Wind

Wind affects the comfort and livability of a patio just as much as the sun does. A gentle breeze blowing across a patio on a hot day is pleasant and refreshing. A strong wind on a cool day is uncomfortable, even downright unpleasant. Fortunately, you can control the wind with wind screens and fences. Properly placed, these structures break up and divert strong winds and channel gentle breezes across a patio.

When studying the wind patterns in your yard, concern yourself with two types: prevailing winds and seasonal breezes. Prevailing wind is the general direction the wind blows in your area. Although that direction may vary from one season to another, it is consistent over your entire region at a given time of year. A seasonal breeze is a more localized wind that occurs only at specific times of day or at certain times during a season.

Both of these winds are affected by the size and position of your house and trees and of those in your neighborhood. Like water, wind flows, always taking the path of least resistance. Even as it moves in

Windscreen/Fence Heights

Solid Fence

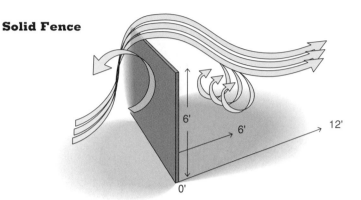

Protection drops off at a distance approximately equal to height of fence

Solid Fence With Screening at Top

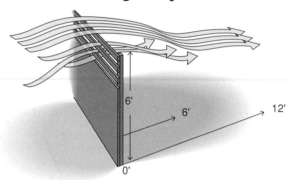

Open screen diffuses the wind and provides wind protection 6'–12' from fence

Solid Fence With Wind Barrier Angled Outward

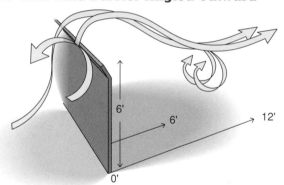

Wind protection near the fence and up to a distance equal to twice its height

Solid Fence With Wind Barrier Angled Inward

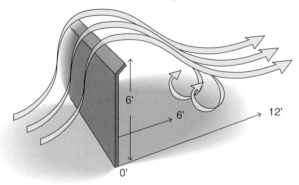

Wind protection up to 8' from fence

a general direction, it spills over objects and breaks around barriers, twisting and turning and forming currents and eddies that create microconditions on a patio. You should study the potential for creating these currents and eddies too. Say, for example, that the wind blows across your patio and into a corner created by the junction of the house and a retaining wall. This corner creates an air dam that forces the wind to eddy, or swirl around, in this pocket and dump any debris it is carrying before it lifts up and moves on. Your goal is to control or channel both the impact of the prevailing wind and the eddies and currents it creates as it moves around your house.

Simply building a solid, high fence won't accomplish this job. Wind-control studies show that wind simply swirls over the top of such obstacles and drops back down at a distance about equal to the height of the fence. This is because the solid fence creates a low-pressure air pocket on the leeward side and causes the wind to become turbulent as it is forced up and over the barrier. The air pocket immediately pulls this turbulent wind down into the protected area. Therefore, instead of a high fence, you need a wind barrier that blocks and diverts the wind without creating turbulence and low-pressure basins.

To determine which type of windbreak provides the best control for your situation, study the effects of the different wind screens and fences shown here. To help you understand your site and the best style for it, place stakes

Patio Microclimates

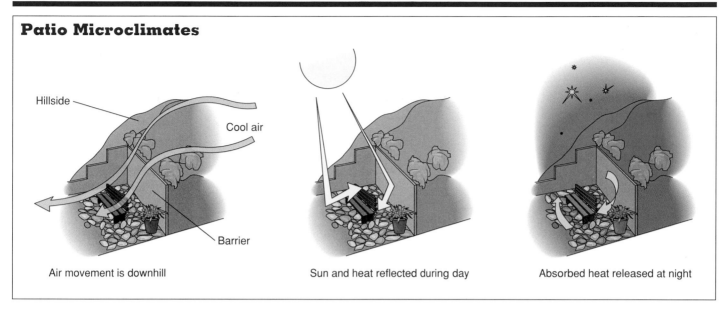

Hillside

Cool air

Barrier

Air movement is downhill

Sun and heat reflected during day

Absorbed heat released at night

with streamers where you want wind protection and note the movement of the streamers on windy days.

Other Weather Conditions

Rain usually follows the same path as prevailing winds. Since you can't block or divert rain, you must provide shelter from it and drainage to carry the water away. For shelter, you can use a solid roof over part of the patio, a temporary roof such as a retractable awning, or a garden structure such as a gazebo. Proper grading usually provides adequate drainage.

Winter weather would seem to be of little concern because you can't use the patio anyway; however, constant freeze/thaw cycles ravage patios and their structures. Consider locating the patio on the leeward side of the house so it is partially protected from this beating.

Creating a Microclimate

As you plan your patio, you're also designing a microclimate. The paving material, for example, determines how much heat from the sun is absorbed or reflected each day. It also affects how light is spread. A light-colored concrete patio reflects a lot of heat, so its surface is comfortably warm, but it also reflects sunlight, making it seem harsh and glaring. On the other hand, dark brick moderates the harshness of bright sunlight and also absorbs the heat. This makes the patio surface uncomfortable to walk on with bare feet during the day, but the stored heat radiates during the cool evening, prolonging the daytime warmth. A patio placed on top of a hill is warmer than one at the base of a hill, because cold air, which is heavier than warm air, flows downhill. At the base of the hill, cold air can get trapped by retaining walls, fences, or house walls, making a patio there quite cold in the evening.

Although this patio is located in a warm climate, the cool colors, natural shade, and partial exposure to gentle breezes make it a welcoming oasis.

Common Patio Siting Options

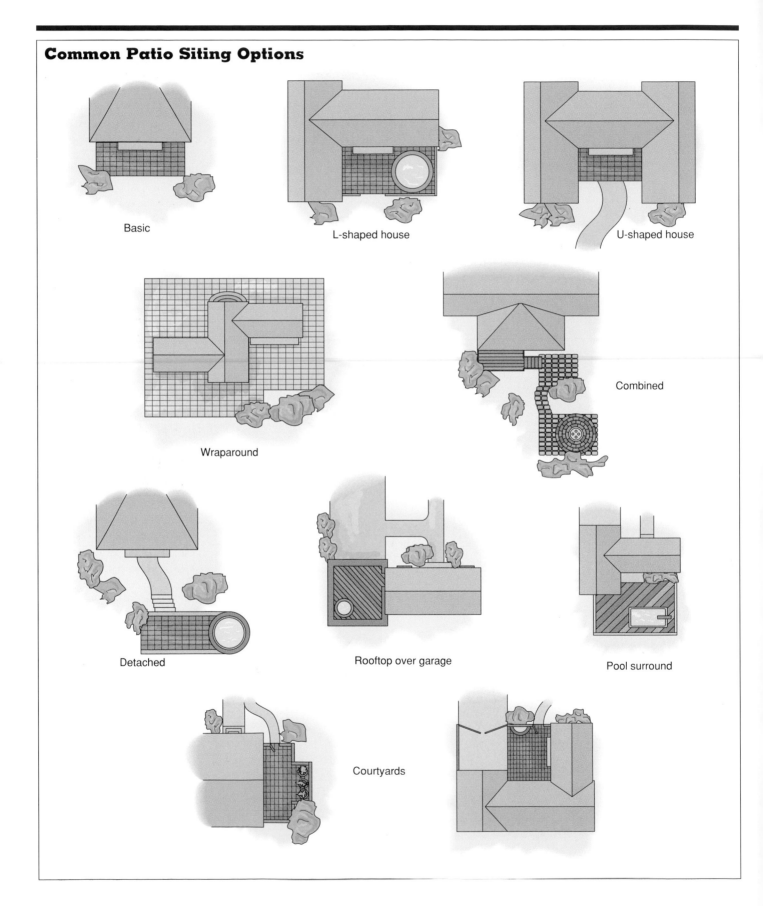

Basic

L-shaped house

U-shaped house

Wraparound

Combined

Detached

Rooftop over garage

Pool surround

Courtyards

Choosing a Final Location

After considering all of these variables, it's time to decide where your patio goes. You have a number of options based on how you want the patio to work for you, the size and terrain of the yard, and your budget. A number of common patio siting options are explained below.

The Basic Attached Patio

This is the typical flat patio attached to the back or side of a house. If the house is L-shaped or U-shaped, the patio may adjoin two or even three walls. Ideally, it measures 12 feet square or larger (but it doesn't have to be square in shape) and is located directly outside the room or rooms from which its function emerges. Often this is the family room, the kitchen, the informal eating area, or a combination of these if they are adjacent to one another.

Design hints: This patio is simple, but it does not have to be plain or dull. Give it style by curving its free edges, creating an interesting pattern in the paving (but be sure it doesn't overwhelm the style of the house), and bordering it with garden beds, low walls, planter boxes, or a combination of these dividers. Tie an attached patio, including any roof, to the architectural style of the home to create a sense of unity.

The Wraparound Patio

This is an ideal layout for a family that wants patio surface off many rooms, or that prefers to clearly separate patio functions such as entertaining and swimming without completely severing the link between them. A wraparound has another big advantage: It makes a house look bigger. It can wrap around two or more sides of the house as family needs and lot size permit. In fact, completely surrounding a house with patio is a good solution when it sits on a very small lot. A wraparound patio works ideally on a flat lot. If the house tucks into a slope or hill, it's best to construct the patio in different levels joined by steps.

Design hints: To create visual interest, curve the patio's edges, round its corners, and border its free sides with garden beds, low walls, planter boxes, or a combination of these. Keep the paving pattern subtle because of the large area it covers. Also, be sure that patio walls, planter boxes, and roof structures complement the architecture of the house. For total coordination, the floor covering in rooms that open onto the patio should have the same background or dominant color as the paving material.

The Detached Patio

Move a patio out into the yard if putting it against the house limits its size or its exposure to sunshine. Although this location eliminates direct step-out access from the house, it gives the patio the natural amenities it requires: sun and openness. A detached patio also has the advantage of being separated from busy household activity; it can become a contemplative retreat, the center of a handsome garden, the adjunct to a swimming pool area, the gateway to a spectacular view, or simply a splendid place to be. Although its surface must be flat, a detached patio can be constructed in levels to accommodate a sloped or hilly lot. Join the levels with steps.

Design hints: Tying the patio to the house architecturally is less crucial here because the two are separate. However, two things are essential for visual success. One is to tie the patio to the house with a direct walkway or path. The other is to pave this walkway and the stoop that leads to it from the house with the same or well-coordinated materials. Also, although they are independent of each other, a detached patio and the house should have the same general tone—formal or informal, traditional or contemporary. Unlike the attached patio, this more isolated structure can support a spectacular patterned surface.

Combined Patios

Combine attached and detached patios to create a large patio complex when yard space permits. Such layouts are common in the Southwest and California, where the climate permits year-round outdoor living. They have the advantage of giving you two patios, one convenient to the house and one out in the yard that can serve any of the functions typically associated with a detached patio (above). This arrangement works especially well when you need a multi-purpose patio but want some separation of functions. This division offers you a bonus, too: It lets you use a greater variety of paving and other patio materials. When yard size and/or shape permit, create a striking complex by building patios at different levels. Whether flat or multi-level, link them with pathways and steps of coordinated materials.

Design hint: All the materials used in both sections should reflect the same general tone, but each patio unit can have a distinct personality. Because of its proximity, however, the attached patio should tie to the house architecturally.

The Pool Surround Patio

Some specific factors come into play when a patio is also the surround for a swimming pool. First, the pool must be located where it gets maximum sunlight. Second, it must be sheltered from the wind. Third, the patio surface must be nonslip as well as attractive in the area immediately adjacent to the pool. Fourth, in order for the pool area to be pleasant for swimmers and nonswimmers alike, the patio must have a shaded section furnished with comfortable seating. Make this area small if there is another patio in the yard. If it is the only patio, however, find a way to tuck these amenities into one of its corners or along its outer edges. How you arrange it depends on the size of the space, which also determines whether you add a hot tub, spa, or decorative pool.

Design hints: Disguise the utilitarian features of a pool by giving its patio surface an interesting pattern. Also, use outcroppings of landscaping materials to soften its edges. An artificial stream cascading over rocks and falling into a decorative pool next to the swimming pool ties all the elements together.

The Courtyard Patio

If you live in a townhouse, condo, patio apartment, brownstone, or even an older house on a narrow city lot, you may not have enough yard space to think in terms of patios the way suburbanites do. That doesn't mean you have to forgo the pleasures of a paved and planted outdoor room. Simply turn the space

Patios in small spaces, such as this front entry, lend themselves to ceramic tile and other refined paving materials. They blend with the home's architecture and interior spaces; they may not be exposed to extreme weather conditions; and the smaller patio area keeps costs down.

you do have, whether it's to the front, back, or side of your dwelling, into a courtyard. If you don't have real walls surrounding the space, create them with fencing or by planting tall hedges. Then build yourself a private oasis by paving the surface and lining the inside of the walls with garden beds. If there isn't room for garden beds, use potted plants, including small trees, to bring greenery and flowers into the space. Don't forget to let plants climb on the courtyard walls. The sound of falling water is especially enchanting in a courtyard. If there isn't space for a small pool with a fountain, use an ornamental wall fountain to create this ambience.

Design hints: Courtyards usually are small, or so long and narrow that they appear small even though their square footage is quite adequate. To cope with this size limitation creatively, keep the paving subdued and the furniture simple, and put the emphasis on plants.

The Roof Patio

A patio placed atop a garage or addition rooftop adjacent to a second-story living space offers a truly private spot for a patio, but you must first consider several important factors. One, can the existing roof structure carry the extra weight of the patio surface, furnishings, and "live loads"? If it can't, reinforce it by nailing new rafters to the existing rafters (this is called "sistering"). Second, can you build some type of privacy wall so the space is safe and secluded? Such a wall changes the exteri-

or appearance of a house, so plan carefully. Third, can you slope the paving sufficiently to allow for adequate drainage into a system of gutters and downspouts? This is an absolute must.

Design hints: Give the patio a feel of lushness by filling its corners and edges with lots of container-grown plants and trees. Use handsome, even colorful, tiles or pavers laid in a striking pattern for the surface. The space can handle strong design because it is isolated from the yard.

Selecting Your Patio Style

At this point, having brought together your wants and the size and contour of your yard, you have decided where the patio will go and its approximate size and shape. Next choose the patio's style. It may be a dramatic architectural statement or a simple garden spot. However, the patio should coordinate with the style of the house, and to some extent with the style of other houses in the neighborhood. This is especially important if your neighborhood has a dominant architectural style reflecting the period in which it was developed or the area's historical or ethnic heritage. The paving and building materials you choose help determine that style (see pages 45 to 55). If you aren't sure which materials to use, indigenous paving and building materials and native plants are always a safe bet. In all of your decisions, keep in mind the basic design principles outlined in the first chapter.

DRAWING YOUR PLAN

You know how you want to use your patio. You have decided on its general location and shape. You have a basic understanding of the necessary alterations to the yard's grade and drainage to accommodate the patio. Now these decisions and details must be translated to paper—to a final plan, or working drawings. Making this plan is much like plotting the furniture layout for a room.

The Drawing Technique

Actually, the site plan can range from a rough sketch to a detailed final drawing. A rough sketch becomes the basis for opening discussions with landscape architects, designers, or contractors, if they will do most of the work. These professionals can help you with every stage of the patio-building process, from design through installation (see page 39). If you plan to do most of the work yourself, you need a detailed final drawing. It becomes your work guide, a basis for estimating materials, and an instruction sheet for any professionals you hire to do part of the job.

Drawing Tools

To make all your drawings, from the base plan to the final site plan and elevations, you need drafting tools and information. The tools include a drafting board, a T square or straightedge, a ruler, a triangle, large sheets (24 inches by 36 inches) of ¼-inch- or ⅛-inch-scale graph paper, a large pad of tracing paper, masking tape, pencils, and an art-gum eraser.

The job is easier if you have an architect's scale, a compass, and a circle template as well. You also need a 50- or 100-foot steel tape measure for measuring features in the yard.

The information you need includes the legal dimensions of your yard and house so you can make an accurate base plan. Get these specifications from your deed map, house plans, plat plan, or a contour plan of the yard. If you don't have at least one of these documents, request them from city hall, the county recorder, or your title or mortgage company. If they don't have them, find the markers in the four corners of your lot and start measuring.

Developing the Drawings

All plans start with a base plan of the yard, which contains all the features of the yard drawn to scale. If you're redoing the whole yard, the base plan must reflect this. However, if you're doing only the portion of the yard that involves the patio and its surrounding landscaping, draw only that section. This lets you increase the scale, making the drawing easier to read. For permit purposes, however, you may need to submit a site plan of the entire lot. Check with the local building department for specific requirements.

The Base Plan

Secure a piece of graph paper to the drafting board with masking tape and draw all the basic dimensions and features of your lot. Be as accurate and as neat as possible. Once you have plotted the lot's boundaries and its fixed elements (such as the house), add the other structures (driveways, sidewalks, and outbuildings) and the garden elements (trees, garden beds, and

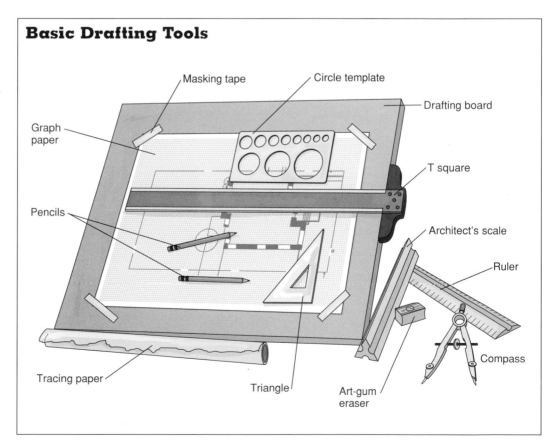

Basic Drafting Tools

Masking tape — Circle template — Drafting board — Graph paper — Pencils — T square — Architect's scale — Ruler — Compass — Tracing paper — Triangle — Art-gum eraser

Sample Base Plan

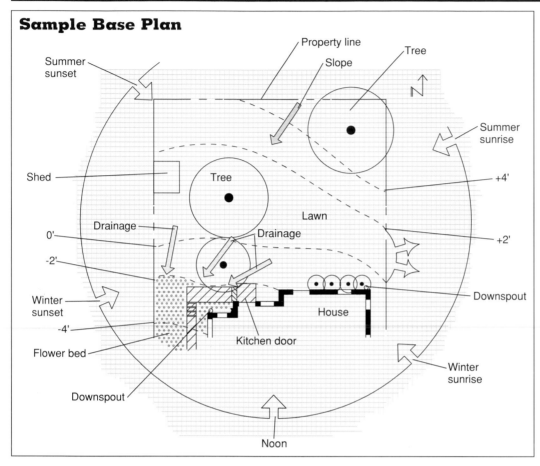

fences) that you intend to keep. When it's done, this base plan gives you the following information at a glance.

• The boundary lines and exact dimensions of the lot. Mark the outline and note the exact dimensions on the graph paper.

• The exact size and placement of the house in relationship to the lot. Mark the locations of all exterior doors and relevant windows. Also indicate the depth of the eaves, the height above ground of all main-floor windows, and the location of the air conditioner and all exterior water faucets, downspouts, and utility meters.

• The direction the house faces. Indicate this by drawing an arrow pointing north.

• The location of existing outbuildings you plan to keep. Draw them to scale in their exact locations on the property.

This patio fits nicely into the gently sloping site because of careful grading, a low retaining wall, and provision for drainage away from the patio.

Measuring Slope

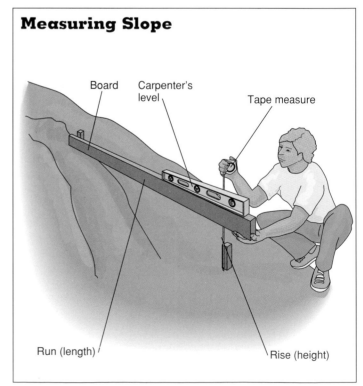

• All utility easements, underground utility lines, and required setbacks. This includes septic tanks and catch basins. Indicate their location and/or boundaries with a dashed line and record the exact dimensions of easements and setbacks.

• The yard's gradients if it is sloped or hilly. Draw these as contour lines, indicating the high and low points. If your yard drains across a neighbor's yard, also indicate how your gradients and theirs connect; you cannot ruin the drainage in your neighbor's yard. If you have an official contour map, use those figures on your plan. If you don't, use a level and straight board to measure the changes in grade (unless the contouring in your yard is complex, in which case, use a builder's transit or hire a surveyor). Take these measurements every 5 feet in stair-step fashion. *Note:* If plotting these lines on your base plan makes it too messy or too confusing, draw them on a separate sheet of tracing paper, then simply lay this sheet over a proposed plan to evaluate its impact on existing grading.

• Existing drainage. Mark the runoff paths that water follows as it flows out of your yard. Note any problems that creates.

• Existing plantings. It's especially important that you draw trees with their mature drip lines indicated by a circle. Do the same for any trees in your neighbors' yards that may one day shade yours, even if they do not shade it today. The crown of a shade tree can easily measure 40 feet in diameter when full grown.

Choosing a Landscape Professional

Many types of professionals are available to help you at every step of the patio-building process, from design to installation. Homeowners often avoid hiring professionals, fearing they are too expensive. No one denies that professionals cost money up front, but consulting the right one at a crucial time will save you the expense of costly, time-consuming mistakes. In that sense, the professionals' services pay for themselves. They pay off in another way too: You get professional-looking design and construction. In order of intensity of training, professionals in this field include landscape architects, landscape designers, landscape contractors, nursery staff, and gardeners. Here is the type of service each of these professionals, plus building contractors, offers you.

• Landscape architect. This is a licensed professional with a college degree in landscape architecture. In most states it is necessary to serve an apprenticeship to a practicing landscape architect and pass a rigorous exam to receive a license. This professional is skilled in creating landscape designs that are original as well as practical and aesthetically pleasing, and is trained in the technical aspects of landscaping, such as grading, drainage, irrigation, and lighting. A landscape architect who does residential design can provide as little or as much service as you want

to buy—from a basic, one-time consultation to give you some ideas, to developing a detailed patio and landscaping design, to evaluating bids and supervising construction. Consider hiring a landscape architect if your lot has difficult terrain or if you need a complex patio plan.

• Landscape designer. Most landscape designers have training in horticulture as opposed to landscape architecture, and they are not required to have a degree or license to work. This lack of specific credentials doesn't mean a landscape designer is less talented than a landscape architect, however; many are just as capable and experienced. Some even have some training in landscape architecture—they just didn't get a degree in it. A landscape designer does many of the same things as a landscape architect, including developing complex designs and planning extensive in-ground work.

• Landscape contractor. This professional carries out the plans developed by the landscape architect, landscape designer, or you. In other words, this contractor and crew actually grade the yard, build the patio and retaining walls, install the swimming pool, and plant the foliage. Often a landscape contractor owns a nursery that supplies the plants. Some states require that a landscape contractor be licensed.

• Nursery staff. Traditionally, nursery workers raise

plants—from flowers to trees—for sale at wholesale and retail. Trained and experienced in horticulture, a nursery staffer may also be a landscape architect, a landscape designer, or a landscape contractor—work in this industry often overlaps because professionals equip themselves to provide a wide range of services to their clients. Although nursery workers are not required to have a college degree or license, they may have both, and their efforts and skills are definitely geared to residential design.

• Gardener. This is the person with the proverbial green thumb. A gardener usually has no formal training, but he or she probably has a lot of knowledge and skill based on years of practical experience. A good gardener can design and even supervise the construction of a simple patio and its landscaping.

• Building contractor. Many general building contractors and most specialists, such as foundation or masonry contractors, are experienced in grading, pouring and finishing concrete, and installing various masonry materials. Although some firms offer full architectural services, the design expertise of most building contractors is limited to structural aspects, such as drainage, thickness of concrete, steel reinforcement, retaining-wall design, and framing of an overhead structure.

Balloon Sketch

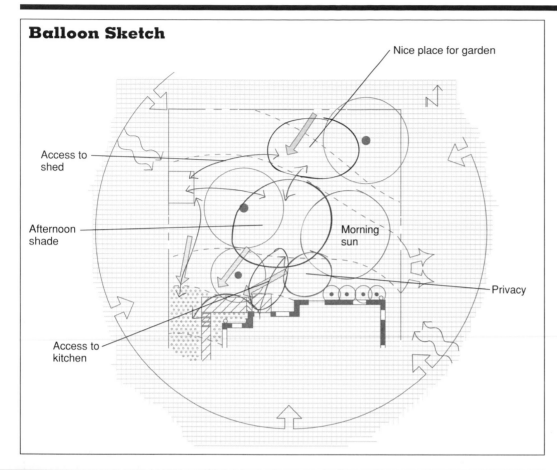

Nice place for garden

Access to shed

Afternoon shade

Morning sun

Access to kitchen

Privacy

It is easy to visualize the main traffic and circulation patterns through this yard. The seating areas have been placed away from the main traffic path, allowing easy passage across the patio without going around obstacles.

• Other details—usually in writing only—that indicate where favorable or unfavorable views exist.

On separate sheets of tracing paper, sketch the shaded and sunlit areas of the yard for different times of day or different times of the year. Simply lay them over a proposed plan to evaluate its sun/shade patterns.

Experimental Drawings

Using the base plan as a guide, make experimental drawings on tracing paper taped over it. These "balloon sketches" are loose drawings in which circles are used to indicate major use areas within the yard. Simply lay a new sheet of tracing paper for each sketch and scribble away. Base the circles on your wish list and the sun, shade, wind, noise, and privacy patterns of the yard. Use this process to try out all your notions, even if you have a firm idea of where you want to locate the patio. Pay particular attention to the circulation patterns you create within the yard. Remember, easy access between the house and patio is imperative; it is also essential between separate patios. Once you start drawing, you may discover that what you planned to do won't work. You may find, for example, that an attached patio needs a trellis for shade but that a trellis would make the adjoining family room too dark. That's why it's good to try out alternative ideas. Make as many balloon sketches as you can.

The graph paper with all the specifications will show

Standard Dimensions

Walkways and Steps

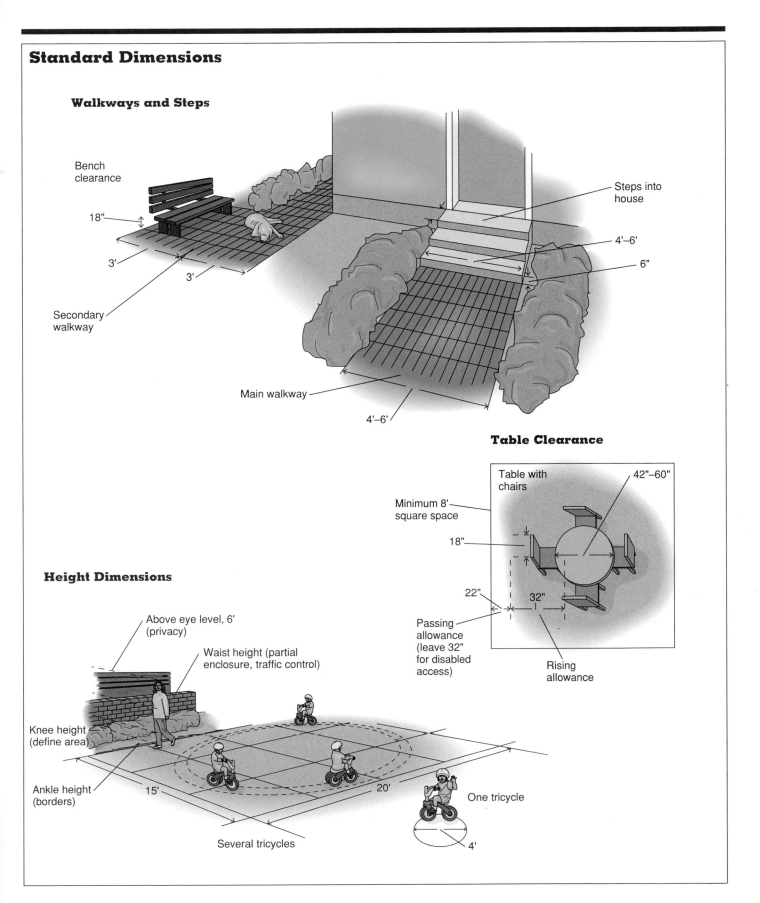

Bench clearance

18"

3'

3'

Secondary walkway

Main walkway

4'–6'

Steps into house

4'–6'

6"

Table Clearance

Table with chairs

42"–60"

Minimum 8' square space

18"

22"

32"

Passing allowance (leave 32" for disabled access)

Rising allowance

Height Dimensions

Above eye level, 6' (privacy)

Waist height (partial enclosure, traffic control)

Knee height (define area)

Ankle height (borders)

15'

20'

Several tricycles

One tricycle

4'

Final Site Plan and Elevations

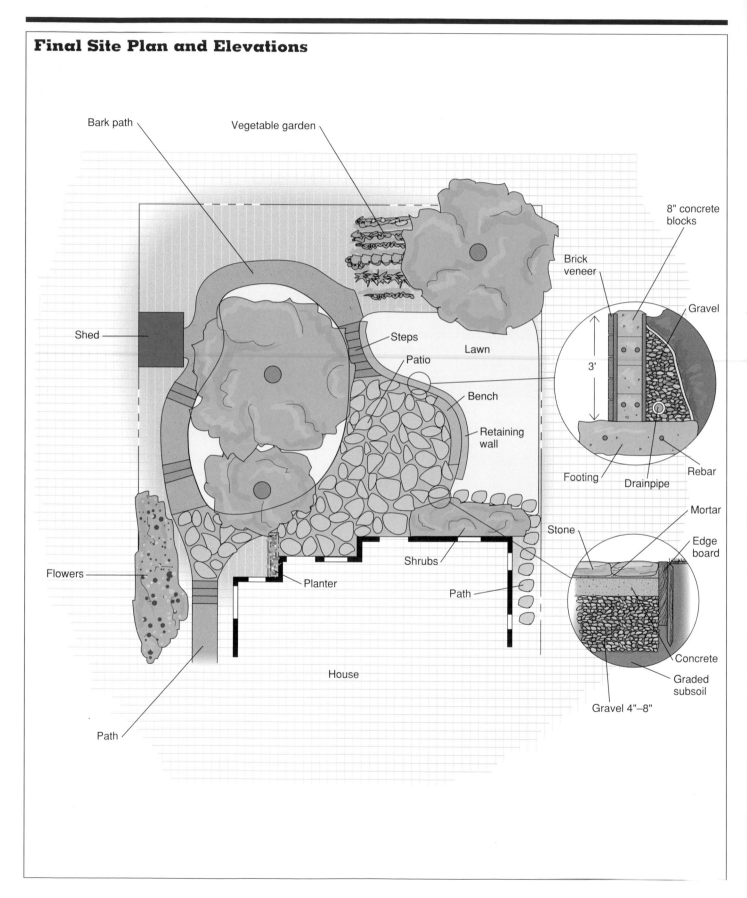

Bark path

Vegetable garden

8" concrete blocks

Brick veneer

Gravel

Shed

Steps

Lawn

Patio

Bench

Retaining wall

3'

Footing

Drainpipe

Rebar

Flowers

Shrubs

Stone

Mortar

Edge board

Planter

Path

Path

House

Concrete

Graded subsoil

Gravel 4"–8"

Test drive your patio design before you make the final drawings. Lay out the boundaries with chalk or garden hoses; use balloons to simulate trees and other visual barriers. Then see how various furniture arrangements work.

through the tracing paper, so you can work close to actual scale even at this preliminary phase. For this reason, it's important to be aware of standard dimensions at this early stage (see page 41). These dimensions are modular measurements that guarantee human comfort and convenience as well as provide the proportion and balance needed for effective design.

Once you have reached a point where your balloon sketch feels right, test your plan in the field. Pace off the proposed patio area. Use shims as temporary stakes to indicate the general boundaries of the paving and of any structures, including garden beds, patio walls, fences, planter boxes, steps, paths, and pools. Then

walk from one staked area to another, imagining that you're actually walking from the house to the patio and carrying out different functions. This test gives you one last chance to modify your basic ideas before beginning the intermediate sketches.

Intermediate Sketches

You probably need one to three intermediate sketches before you are ready to make the final drawings. These are bird's-eye views similar to the layouts you make when furnishing a room. Again, you work on tracing paper, the first sheet over the last balloon sketch, the second sheet over the first intermediate sketch, and so on,

until you are ready to make the final drawings. You get more precise with each sketch, firming up fine details as you work. When everything is in place, you are ready to make the final drawings.

The Final Drawings

The final drawings, also called working drawings, should include at least a "plan view"— a detailed aerial perspective of the patio itself and nearby landscaping features. The plan view should show all the details important to constructing the patio and any other landscaping features; be sure to include a cross section of the patio foundation. If your design involves building

divider walls, retaining walls, steps, or other raised structures, draw elevations (cross sections) of these to scale too. You may also need to draw a site plan of the entire lot, showing where the new patio will be located.

To make the plan view, tape your last intermediate sketch over the base plan. Tape a clean sheet of tracing paper on top of the two and make your final drawing. Make it as neat as possible and label each element in the design.

Draw elevations as cross sections that show how the structure is to be built. Using the same tools you used to make your preliminary sketches, draw them to scale in a flat, vertical plane as seen from a straight-on perspective.

CHOOSING PATIO MATERIALS

All patio materials are naturally handsome and capable of producing an attractive patio, so it may seem that any type will do. However, choosing the right material isn't that simple. Effective design requires careful consideration of each material in terms of color, texture, and pattern, as well as any regional or historical associations it may have. Furthermore, you need to consider how the patio will be used—for example, is the material suitable for tricycles? And you must keep in mind the microclimate—will moss grow on it too readily? Finally, there may be technical issues to consider, such as the type of foundation the paving requires, or whether the material is appropriate for a do-it-yourself installation. This chapter, which provides a basic introduction to the most popular types of patio materials, will enable you to carefully evaluate each in terms of its aesthetic properties and structural characteristics.

Among these stacks of bricks you might find your patio. When you visit a masonry yard, bring along a tape measure, some color samples of your house's exterior, and samples of plants or other landscaping materials that are prominant in your yard.

CONCRETE: THE BASIC MATERIAL

Patio materials come in such a multitude of styles, sizes, shapes, colors, and compositions that you may not know where to start. After learning some general guidelines for choosing a paving material, you might want to explore concrete first, because it is the most basic and versatile patio material.

How to Choose Materials

A patio's hard surfaces—its pavement and walls—constitute its fundamental structure and can consume as much as 75 percent of your budget. They also determine its basic style. For these reasons it is important to choose materials carefully. To make the job easier, compile a list of everything that you want the patio materials to do. The following points will help you organize the list.

• Consider the mood and style of the patio. A patio's paving is a unifying element that sets its mood. Do you want it to be traditional or contemporary? Formal or informal? Bold or subdued? Warm or cool? Grand or intimate?

• Consider features of your home or landscape that the patio should blend with, such as walkways or steps. Are there indigenous materials you would like to incorporate?

• How will the patio be used? Some surfaces are particularly suitable for certain activities, such as dancing or children's play. Will you prepare and serve food and drinks frequently that may stain the surface?

• Consider the weather. Some materials become slippery when wet; others absorb moisture that may cause cracking in a hard freeze. What if the material changes color dramatically when it is wet? Would moss become a problem? When the sun shines, do you prefer that the patio reflect the heat or absorb as much heat as possible? What about glare?

• Are there structural issues to consider, such as frost heaves, unstable soil, drainage, a floor level that needs to be matched, or underground utilities that require access? Is there an existing patio that needs to be removed, or is it sound enough to simply pave over it?

• Consider logistics. Will you build the patio yourself? Are there access problems that might make some materials harder to transport than others? Will the patio be built in stages or all at once?

• Will the patio include walls or raised planters? If your choice of paving material isn't suitable for building walls, you'll need to choose a wall material that complements or coordinates with it.

• What are the costs of materials, delivery, and their installation?

Keep your list in mind as you read about the seven categories of patio materials.

Poured Concrete

Poured concrete is the basic patio material. It forms an excellent foundation for most other materials and is a simple, versatile, and economical finished surface, especially when you need to cover large areas. Poured concrete can be worked into almost any shape and can take a number of interesting surface finishes. It can be divided into sections or bordered; contrasting materials, such as pavers, bricks, wood dividers, or tiles, can be incorporated into the patio design. Concrete can also be used to make a contrasting-border around other paving materials. And should you eventually tire of a concrete patio, it provides a superb base for a new patio surface of brick, stone, or tile set in mortar.

Concrete does have some disadvantages, especially for the do-it-yourselfer. One is that it must be mixed to exact specifications. Another is that it must be poured and finished quickly. Also, you need at least one helper. The essential site preparation—grading, installing the base materials, and building the forms—is tedious, and if you don't do it

Concrete can be used in many interesting and unexpected ways. The tile pattern of this patio was stamped into the surface of the fresh concrete and then stained to the finish color. Notice how the patio slopes away from the pool toward the drain.

correctly, you risk a buckled or cracked slab. (Concrete is always vulnerable to cracking, but control joints, which are grooves made at intervals in the surface, will minimize it; see page 75.) Its surface becomes hot and glaring if unshaded, and slippery when wet unless it is textured. Concrete's tendency to expand is also a consideration; you must plan expansion joints to avoid damage to a house foundation, for instance.

Types of Concrete

Use a general-purpose concrete made with Type I, IA, II, IIA, III, or IIIA portland cement. These are general-purpose portland cements suitable for paving patios and sidewalks. The *A* suffix indicates a portland cement used to make the air-entrained concrete needed in regions subject to freezing weather (air-entrained concrete has an additive that makes it more tolerant of freezing). If you order concrete ready-mixed, the dealer mixes the right amount in the correct proportions for your climate and use. If you choose to mix it yourself, using bulk dry materials or a dry ready-mixed concrete, you have to make these determinations yourself. Follow the manufacturer's instructions exactly. More detailed instructions appear in the following chapter.

Concrete Finishes

Applying a decorative surface treatment gives concrete improved traction and a pleasing texture. There are nine finishes from which to choose.

• Exposed aggregate. This is the most popular concrete finish. Its pebbly surface is slightly rugged, naturally colorful, and highly durable.

• Troweled finish. A swirled texture made with a trowel, this finish gives the patio an interesting texture and good traction.

• Broomed finish. This attractive, nonslip texture is created by pulling damp brooms across freshly floated or troweled concrete.

• Travertine finish. This handsome surface resembles travertine marble. It is not recommended for regions with freezing weather.

• Rock salt finish. This is a slightly pitted, roughened surface created by rolling rock salt (ordinary water-softener salt) into the concrete. It produces excellent traction, but is not recommended for areas with freezing temperatures.

• Semismooth finish. This is a slightly roughened texture produced with a wood float. This surface is recommended when you need good skid resistance and when floating is the final finish.

• Smooth finish. You achieve this effect by troweling the floated surface with a metal trowel. Slippery when wet, it is not recommended for patios and sidewalks.

• Stamped-pattern finish. Geometric designs stamped into partially set concrete make it resemble materials such as brick, cobblestone, flagstone, or ashlar (veneer stone). You can do this yourself, but a contractor will give you more professional-looking results.

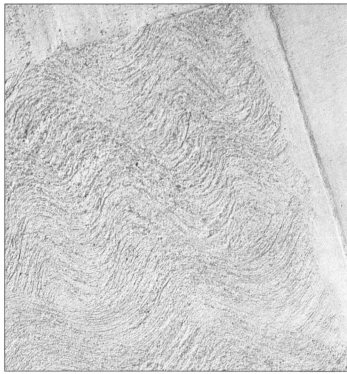

Top: Concrete with an exposed aggregate finish. Bottom: Concrete with a broom finish.

• Hand-tooled finish. This surface is achieved by scoring random patterns in partially set concrete with a tool or stylus, before and after the slab has been floated.

In addition to texturing the surface, you can color concrete; see page 83 for detailed information.

Purchasing Concrete

A ready-mix dealer offers the most convenient and economical source of concrete.

Concrete is sold by the cubic yard (27 cubic feet), and a supplier will deliver any quantity greater than 1 cubic yard. It is important to order exactly how much you need. You pay for what you order, even if you don't need it all. To determine how much concrete you need, follow the instructions below. Here's an example of the calculation using a patio that measures 12 feet wide by 20 feet long; the slab is to be 4 inches thick: *12 × 20 = 240; 240 × ⅓ (4 inches = ⅓ of a foot) = 80 cubic feet. 80 ÷ 27 = 2.96 cubic yards. 2.96 + .296 (10 percent waste allowance) = 3.25 cubic yards ordered.*

For information on ordering or mixing concrete, see page 77.

Calculating Area

To figure the square feet of rectangular or circular areas, use the formulas you learned in school: for rectanglar, length multiplied by width; for circular, 3.14 multiplied by the radius squared. Complex shapes can be figured by drawing them on graph paper with each square representing 1 square foot—count all the squares within the patio area, including partial squares larger than half a square.

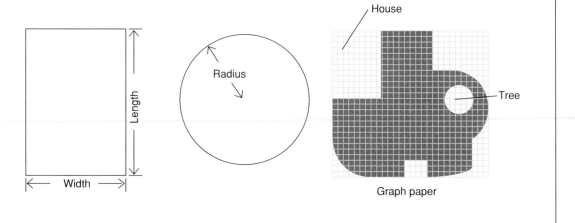

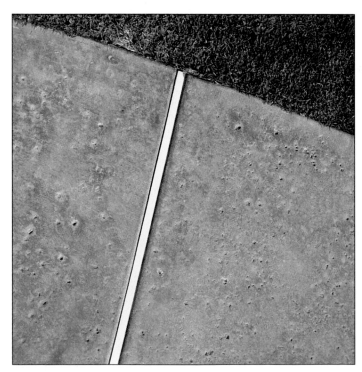

Concrete with a pitted finish created by rock salt.

Concrete with a stamped finish and variegated stain.

BRICK & PAVERS: THE MODULAR CHOICE

Brick has a long tradition as a paving material for patios, from ancient times to the present. More recently, interlocking concrete pavers, which offer many of the same advantages as brick, have also become popular choice. Both are excellent for do-it-yourself installations.

Brick

Brick is the old standby—the most adaptable, attractive, and popular patio paving material. Its beautifully textured surface comes in a wide range of colors; it ranges in style from earthy to refined. In addition, the shape of brick allows it to be laid in an infinite number of interesting patterns. It can be used to build walls and other structures, such as columns, as well as for a border material. All these qualities make it suitable for use with most architectural styles, traditional to contemporary, although it is most closely associated with traditional styles, both formal and informal.

Brick offers the do-it-yourself patio builder many advantages. It is fairly simple to install, and its size makes it easy to handle. It is widely available and, if a delivery is not feasible, it can be transported in small quantities. A brick patio is durable and requires little maintenance except occasionally weeding the joints and refilling them.

Brick does have drawbacks. It is more expensive than most other paving materials. It looks awkward if not laid in a precise pattern. Occasionally, some bricks heave and have to be reset. Also, brick can become slick with moss in humid or heavily shaded areas.

Common Installation Methods

Once you establish your rhythm, brick goes down with ease. Brick is laid by three methods. The most common is brick-in-sand, an easy paving technique that also produces a low-upkeep patio. It is not a permanent installation and may be subject to uneven settlement. Installing brick in dry mortar is a variation on the brick-in-sand method. Although it locks the bricks more firmly in place, it still lacks a stable foundation. For a permanent installation, brick is laid in mortar over a concrete-slab foundation. The following chapter contains step-by-step instructions for each. Before you begin, however, you need to know more about brick as a paving material.

Types of Brick

You face a bewildering array of choices—more than 10,000 potential combinations of sizes, shapes, colors, and textures—when you shop for brick. Start winnowing down the selection with this fact: Common brick, face brick, and paving brick are best for paving patios.

Common Brick

Also called building brick or standard brick, common brick is the least expensive. It is not uniform in shape or color, and its imperfections give it a natural appearance that is ideal for patios.

There are three types of common brick: sand-mold, wire-cut, and clinker. Sand-mold brick is slightly larger on one side and has rounded edges and a smooth texture. Wire-cut brick has sharp edges, a rough texture, and a slightly pitted face. Clinker brick has flashed patches and a rough surface, caused by overburning.

You can obtain these common types new or used. The rustic appearance of used bricks makes an attractive informal patio. However, common bricks more than 30 to 40 years old are too porous

Centuries of bricklaying have produced many interesting patterns that lend themselves to backyard patios—from sedate, regimented grids to bold circles.

Brick Paving Patterns

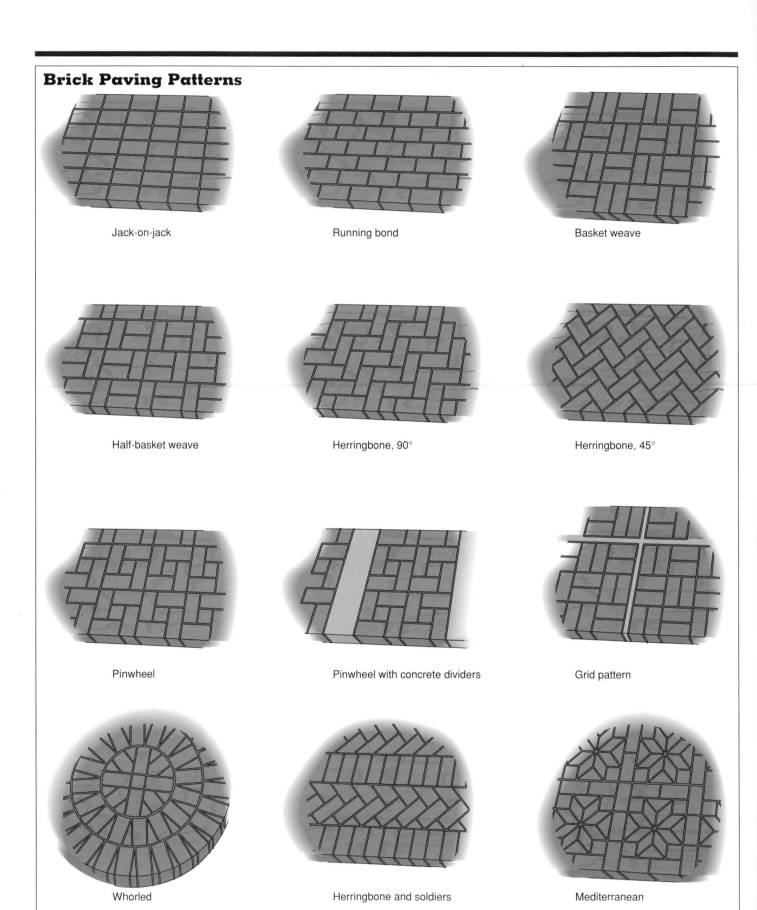

Jack-on-jack

Running bond

Basket weave

Half-basket weave

Herringbone, 90°

Herringbone, 45°

Pinwheel

Pinwheel with concrete dividers

Grid pattern

Whorled

Herringbone and soldiers

Mediterranean

to stand up in regions with freezing winter weather. Genuine used bricks are expensive because they must be cleaned and are in high demand. As a result, there are also new "used" bricks manufactured by tumbling the bricks to chip their edges and splashing them with mortar and paint.

Common bricks come graded according to their ability to withstand cold weather. Only two grades are acceptable for use on patios.

•SW (severe weathering) brick is suitable for patios in all climates, including areas with subzero winters. It is the most expensive common brick.

•MW (moderate weathering) brick is suitable for patios in areas with subfreezing, but not subzero, weather. It is less expensive than SW common brick.

Face Brick

Face brick is used to face buildings and walls. Available new or used, it is uniform in size, shape, and color and has a smooth, defect-free surface. The best quality brick, it also is the most expensive. Face brick is not stronger than common brick, but it is more weather-resistant. The smooth surface also makes it more slippery when wet.

Paving Brick

Composed of special clays and fired at higher temperatures for longer periods, paving brick is stronger than common brick, which is why it typically is half the thickness of standard bricks. Designed and sized for mortarless installation, it is ideal for building brick-on-sand patios.

How Brick Is Sized

Bricks are modular and sized in 4-inch increments, so they fit together regardless of how they are placed. However, terminology and measurements vary widely. For example, the term *modular* is sometimes used to denote a specific size of brick, which is different from *standard* bricks.

Typically, standard or modular bricks are used for patios; these have a stated measurement of 4 by 8 by 2¼ inches or 2⅔ inches. However, this may be the brick's nominal measurement, which includes the thickness of an average mortar joint. Ask the dealer if the stated size is the nominal or the actual size. Don't try to determine the size by measuring a brick with a ruler. It's common for individual bricks in a run to vary as much as ½ inch from standard dimensions.

Paving brick is an exception to this rule. It is referred to by its exact dimension—4 by 8 inches—because it is designed for mortarless installation.

Brick Colors and Textures

Most bricks get their color from the mineral oxides in the clay from which they are

made. When the bricks are fired, these oxides turn their natural color, any of a wide range of warm, earthen tones.

Brick finishes, or textures, range from smooth to rough. Choose a texture that provides good traction and a comfortable walking surface—a sand finish is a good choice. Don't use glazed bricks on patios because they are slippery when they get wet.

Brick Patterns

Once you have chosen a brick, select the pattern, called a bond, that you want to use. As you make this decision, consider the following points.

•What type of joint will you use—an open joint that has some space between the bricks, or a closed joint that butts the bricks tightly together? Open joints become a part of the pattern; butt joints produce a smooth, uniform appearance. Open joints let you adjust for the natural size variations in common bricks. If a butt joint is essential, use a mortarless paving brick.

•How difficult is the pattern to lay? Intricate patterns require a lot of brick cutting as well as precision in laying.

•How will the pattern look on the patio? Easy patterns such as jack-on-jack

and running bond become monotonous on large patios. Intricate patterns like Mediterranean create confusion on a small patio.

Put interest into the patio pattern. Some effective ways to do this include changing the direction of a bond, combining patterns, mixing or alternating brick colors within a pattern, adding a decorative border, or incorporating another material such as wood or concrete into the scheme. To avoid problems, test your design by laying it out on graph paper or by cutting out cardboard "bricks" and laying them on the ground.

Ordering Brick

Brickyards and landscape- or building-supply companies have the best selection of bricks. If you want used brick, try salvage yards.

To order bricks, first determine the square footage of your patio (see page 48). Then, to estimate the number of bricks you need, allow 5 bricks per square foot of patio surface. Add 5 percent to the total to allow for waste. Have the brick dealer recalculate the total to ensure accuracy.

Bricks are sold individually or in blocks of 100 or 500 units. Since a block of 500 bricks weighs 1 ton, ask the dealer to have the bricks delivered on a pallet; the expense is far less than the cost of the damage done by dumping them off a truck.

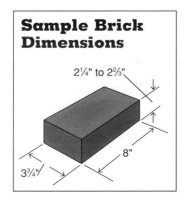

Sample Brick Dimensions

2¼" to 2⅔"

8"

3¾"

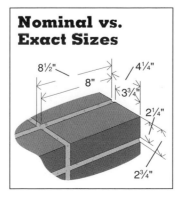

Nominal vs. Exact Sizes

8½"

8"

4¼"

3¾"

2¼"

2¾"

Interlocking Concrete Pavers

Interlocking concrete pavers are manufactured expressly for use in paving patios and walks. They are available in an endless variety of shapes, sizes, colors, and textures. There's an appropriate paver for every architectural style. Durable, stable, and less expensive than other materials, they make broad, unbroken patio surfaces. Some colored pavers have shallow pigment; over time, bare concrete shows through. To avoid this, buy pavers that are permeated with color throughout.

Installing Pavers

Concrete pavers are designed for mortarless installation in a sand bed. Their interconnecting shapes give them such stability that the mortarless surface remains intact, even under stress, heavy loads, and freezing weather. Pavers with beveled or chamfered edges are particularly stable. Use the instructions for installing a brick-in-sand patio in the next chapter as a guide to installing concrete pavers.

Types of Concrete Pavers

Pavers are made from extremely dense concrete that is pressure-formed into various shapes, including turf-retaining pavers, which have holes in which to plant ground covers or grass. There's a wide variation in price, depending on size, thickness, and texture. You can cast your own pavers using forms and other materials supplied in a kit, but they won't be as strong as commercial pressure-formed pavers.

Paver Characteristics

Pavers vary in size as much as in shape—from 1½ inches to 3⅛ inches thick. Pavers up to 2½ inches thick work well on patios. There's a broad choice of earth-toned colors, including grays and off-whites.

Paver Patterns

Because a paver's shape creates the pattern on a patio, choose it carefully. Pay particular attention to its scale in proportion to the patio size. The pattern created by small pavers becomes too busy or gets lost on a large patio. Likewise, the pattern created by large pavers dwarfs a small patio.

Their modularity makes it possible to lay pavers, especially rectangular ones, in the same basic patterns in which you lay bricks. The most effective patterns are running bond, half-basket weave, basket weave, pinwheel, and herringbone (see page 50). Take care that the pattern doesn't become too busy. Use contrasting material to relieve the monotony of large expanses of simple rectangular pavers.

Ordering Pavers

Pavers are sold by the individual piece by building-supply outlets, home centers, and nurseries. Landscape-supply dealers and manufacturers sell them by the square foot. Use the methods outlined for ordering brick on page 51 to figure the patio's square footage. If your chosen paver is the size of standard brick, multiply the square footage by 5 and add 5 percent for waste to get the amount you need. Otherwise, ask the dealer to calculate the amount you need. Pavers come packaged in full cubes, or bands, sufficient to pave 16 lineal feet. The dealer will convert your patio's square footage to lineal feet and then round off to the next highest band. Ask for an additional 5 percent to cover waste.

Concrete pavers, installed over a bed of compacted sand and butted tightly together, produce a stable, durable, and economical patio surface. The beveled edges of the pavers allow slight variations in alignment.

STONE, TILE, ADOBE & WOOD

If one of your requirements for a paving material is that it be unique or even exotic, consider stone, tile, adobe, or wood. These materials are less common than concrete or brick, but each has distinct advantages for certain types of patios.

Stone: The Natural Choice

Stone is the oldest and most rugged of all the paving materials. It is natural, beautiful, colorful, and plentiful. If you use a stone indigenous to your region, you can't go wrong in terms of style—and few areas of the country are without wonderful native stone. The only requirement is that it can be cut into flat pieces—dimensional tiles for formal patio floors, and flagstones (or cobblestones) for informal patios. Stone, like brick, has the added advantage of being suitable for constructing walls.

Methods of Installation

Technically, stone is the only material that can be laid directly on stable soil without first grading a base. Simply remove the turf under the stone and drop it in place. However, it works best when laid in sand, dry mortar, or wet mortar. The irregular thickness of stone means it must be seated in at least 2 inches of sand or 1 inch of mortar. Use the instructions for installing a brick-in-sand patio (page 70) as a guide to installing a flagstone or cobblestone patio.

Types of Stone

The most common stone used for paving patios is flagstone (cobblestones are occasionally seen). This name doesn't identify a type of stone; rather, it describes its shape: flat, thin, and irregular. Good stones for paving are native limestone and sandstone; granite, bluestone, basalt, and other igneous rocks; and slate.

Flagstones do have some disadvantages. Sandstone and limestone are porous, so they absorb water and continue to break up as the water freezes and thaws. Conversely, dense stones don't absorb water and hence become slippery when wet. Most natural stones tend to be rough and uneven; their surface is poor for outdoor furniture and difficult to keep clean. Finally, stone is expensive. It costs 5 to 10 times as much as brick or concrete, partly because it's so heavy. Using indigenous or native stone helps avoid exorbitant shipping costs. Many quarries now cut the dense stones, such as slate, into rectangular and square tiles with relatively even faces, making them easier to ship, handle, and install.

Stone Sizes and Colors

Flagstone comes cut in standard sizes, or uncut in irregular shapes. Cut flagstones are modular and sized in 4-inch increments so they can be fit together in interesting patterns. Irregular flagstones are beautiful but must be laid out carefully to avoid creating a chaotic, patchwork look. Flagstones range from ½ inch to 2 inches thick—thicknesses that work well on residential patios. Don't try to use ashlar—stone cut to veneer walls and buildings—because it is too thick.

These flagstones, volcanic in origin, lend a casual, natural feeling to this patio and give it a distinctive regional identity.

Stone Patterns

Use cut flagstones of one size to make a uniform pattern or use multiple sizes to make a random pattern. Irregular and semiregular flagstones are far more difficult to lay out successfully. If you plan to lay them in a sand bed, make trial layouts until you get the look you want; then install permanently.

Ordering Stone

Purchase stone from a landscape stone dealer. Professional landscape contractors buy it by the ton, but you can buy it by the square foot if you prefer. For reference, 1 ton of flagstone covers 80 to 120 square feet of patio surface. Use the method outlined for ordering brick (page 51) to determine your patio's square footage. Ask the dealer about the cost of delivery, which is not included in the price of the stone. Unless you have a strong back and access to a sturdy truck or trailer, having it delivered makes sense in every way.

Unglazed Tile: Uniquely Elegant

Handsome, colorful ceramic tiles create a uniformly patterned surface and have the advantage of a wider choice of colors than other materials.

Because they are square, it is harder to lay ceramic tiles in patterns similar to those achieved with brick. Instead, rely on contrasting grout lines

and the natural beauty of the tile to achieve an interesting patio surface, or use tile for borders and accent strips for other materials.

There are four basic types of unglazed outdoor tiles: patio tiles, quarry tiles, pavers, and synthetic stones. (Some people consider adobe to be another type of unglazed tile, although it is sun dried and not fired in a kiln. Adobe is covered in its own section below.) Patio, or terra-cotta, tiles are molded, fired ceramic tiles; their earthy colors and irregular shapes and surfaces create a peasant mood. Quarry tiles are molded, fired ceramic tiles in colors and shapes that resemble quarried stone. Pavers also are molded, fired ceramic tiles, in bigger sizes for paving large areas. Pavers come in a variety of earth tones; styles range from rustic and informal, such as the familiar Mexican pavers, to crisp and modern. Synthetic stones are lightweight, fired ceramic tiles that resemble such rock as granite and sandstone; they are similar in composition to the veneer stones used to face walls. Available in warm, earthen colors and natural, neutral tones, they measure 6 inches square or larger; 12 inches square is the most popular size. All these tiles go well on southwestern– and Southern California–style patios, formal or informal.

Use only unglazed ceramic tiles for a patio surface. Glazed tiles are slippery, even when dry, and they're deadly when wet. For the surest, safest traction, use unglazed, textured tiles specified for outdoor use.

Methods of Installation

All ceramic tiles must be set in mortar on a concrete slab that is sound and absolutely level. Although ceramic tile is recommended for warm climates, it can be installed in cold climates that do freeze, but only according to a set of exact standards established by the Tile Council of America. These regulations are so complicated that they prohibit do-it-yourself installation.

Ordering Tile

Purchase tile by the square foot, using the method outlined for ordering brick (page 51) to determine the square footage. Because most tiles are 6 by 6 inches or 12 by 12 inches, figuring the exact number of tile you need isn't complicated.

Adobe: The Fun Mud

Adobe is a sun-dried (not fired) brick or tile made of clay, straw, and an asphalt stabilizer. It has a rustic, earthy quality and makes a durable patio surface. Although adobe as a material is indigenous to the Southwest and associated with the southwestern style, the tiles made today are suitable for use anywhere in the country because they are asphalt stabilized. However, adobe tile is manufactured exclusively in the Southwest and is extremely costly to ship elsewhere in the country.

Installing Adobe

Adobe pavers measure 6 by 12 inches and 12 by 12 inches and are 2½ inches thick. Set them in a sand bed. Use the instructions for a brick-in-sand patio (page 70) as a guide.

Ordering Adobe

The best approach is to buy directly from adobe manufacturers. The tiles are sold by the square foot. Use the method for ordering brick (page 51) to determine the square footage. Because the tiles measure 1 square foot (or half that), figuring your needs is not difficult.

Wood: The Patio As Platform

Although wood is most often thought of as a deck material, it can be laid on grade as a patio pavement. It's available in round slices that look like stepping stones, blocks that look like old bricks, decking squares that look like parquet tiles, and decking boards. Slices and blocks usually are embedded in the earth (use the instructions for installing a brick-in-sand patio on page 70). Squares and boards are mounted on low frames built directly on grade. The naturalness and warmth of wood make it an ideal paving material for all types of informal patios, traditional and contemporary. It is also an excellent border and divider material.

Wood is the least permanent of all the paving materials, even if it's pressure-treated and is of a rot- and insect-resistant species such as heart redwood, cedar, or cypress. Woodlike products have recently been developed for

outdoor decking that are manufactured from recycled plastics; some are composites made from a blend of wood fibers and plastic resins. This alternative material comes in dimensioned boards, just like ordinary lumber. These boards can be sawn, fastened, and finished like lumber. The advantages of this material are that it is dimensionally stable, it is more durable than wood—a particular advantage for patios that hug the ground—and it is made from recycled materials. On the negative side, it lacks the grain pattern of natural wood, and is no less expensive.

Top: Glazed decorative tiles and white flowers provide striking accents to the unglazed pavers of this southwestern patio. Bottom: A ground-hugging deck is a variation on the patio theme. The materials must be suitable for ground contact.

EDGING MATERIALS

Except where a patio abuts walls, planters, and steps, it requires an edging to keep loose-laid materials in place and to keep grass, plants, and soil where they belong. Edgings also serve a decorative function by providing clean, crisp borders and, where contrasting materials are used, adding interesting design effects.

Choosing an Edging Material

The most common do-it-yourself edging materials are brick, wood, stone, concrete, and plastic strips. When considering materials for an edging, be aware of such aspects as contrast (to emphasize lines and shapes or to relieve large expanses of paving material), maintenance (some lawn trimmers require a straight edge), safety (smooth versus jagged edges), durability, and ease of installation. To help you evaluate the options, the following section summarizes the various installation techniques. For additional information, see page 69.

Brick

The brick-in-soil edging is the easiest to build. Place the bricks on end (bricks so placed

A patio edging at the same level as the lawn makes it easy to trim the grass.

are called "soldiers") or flat and at right angles to the patio. Flat bricks should be set in concrete; soldiers may not need concrete footings if they extend below grade far enough to butt against the patio's base material.

To set bricks in concrete, first build a form around the patio, using stakes and long lengths of 2-by lumber. The form should be deep enough for at least 4 inches of concrete and one brick laid flat, and wide enough to accommodate the length of one brick (or width, if you lay them lengthwise). The top of the form should be level with the patio surface. Fill the form with enough concrete so that if a brick is laid on top of it, the brick will be flush with the top of the form. Place the bricks into the wet concrete, butting them together. Set them with a rubber mallet so the tops are level with the form. Allow the concrete to cure for five days before removing the forms and packing soil around it. For a variation on this installation, angle the bricks, laying them against one another so their corners extend above the patio to make a serrated or scalloped edging.

Wood

Build wood edgings with highly rot- and insect-resistant species, such as heart redwood, cedar, or cypress, or pressure-treated lumber. The typical wood edging is made with 4×4 or 6×6 beams or with 2×4s or 2×6s on edge. The mason's twine with which you have outlined the patio perimeter marks the inner

edges of the edging. Dig a narrow trench deep enough and wide enough to hold the wood, its top edge aligning with the patio surface. If you are using beams, place them in the trench, end to end, aligning their inner faces with the twine. Secure them to the ground with ½-inch galvanized-steel pipe. If you are using lumber on edge, line the trench with 12-inch-long 1×3 or 2×3 stakes placed 4 feet apart. Set the boards against the stakes, with their inner faces aligning with the mason's twine. Use wallboard screws to secure the studs to the stakes and to each other at the corners. Pack soil around the outside.

You also can use 12-inch-long round posts ranging from 4 to 6 inches in diameter, or 4×4 or 6×6 beams cut into 12-inch-long post lengths, to make standing wood trim that rises 4 to 6 inches above the patio surface. Secure these posts to the ground by setting them in concrete footings or by drilling holes in each end and driving 2-foot lengths of ½-inch galvanized-steel pipe through them and into the ground.

Stone

Flagstones, boulders, or cobblestones make a rugged and natural-looking patio edge. As with flat bricks, stone edgings should be installed on a concrete footing—the stones can be placed directly onto the wet concrete or set in mortar over hardened concrete. Do a test layout of the stones before you do the permanent installation in concrete or mortar.

Patio Edgings

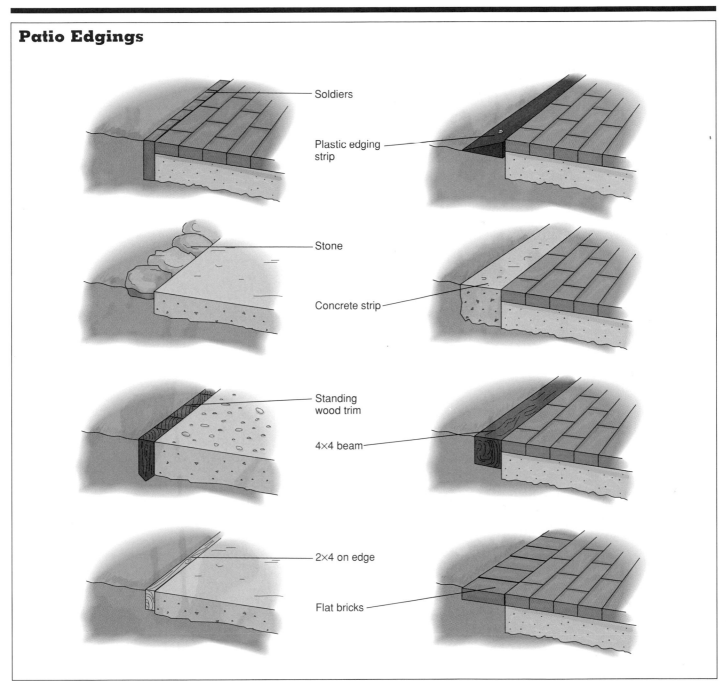

Soldiers

Plastic edging strip

Stone

Concrete strip

Standing wood trim

4×4 beam

2×4 on edge

Flat bricks

Concrete

A concrete edging flush with the ground, called a "mowing strip," is fairly easy to build and provides a smooth, clean patio edge. The width can vary, but most mowing strips are 4 to 6 inches wide. Using stakes and long lengths of 2×4 lumber, build a form along the perimeter of the patio; the top of the form should be level with the patio surface. To make curves, use bender-board or similar thin boards and double them up. This is one of the few places where hand-mixing concrete from dry ready-mix is economical. For instructions on mixing concrete, see page 77. Screed the concrete level with the top of the form. Run an edging tool along the outside form board to give the concrete a rounded edge. Finish the surface as you would for concrete paving (see page 47 and page 80).

Plastic Strips

Plastic edging strips give do-it-yourselfers an easy and convenient way to edge a patio. These are concealed edgings, so they don't add a decorative element to the patio, but they are practical and economical to use. Follow the manufacturer's installation instructions.

CONSTRUCTION BASICS

You are about to embark on one of the most satisfying do-it-yourself projects: building a patio. This process may seem to be simply a matter of installing a handsome paving material. However, a patio is only as handsome as it is stable. That means it must be set on a sound, well-drained base, and its paving must be correctly installed. With an eye to these critical needs, this chapter presents site preparation techniques for any kind of patio. It then takes you step-by-step through the construction process for installing the three most common types of patios: brick-in-sand, poured concrete, and brick-in-mortar. In addition, because most homes built in the past fifty years have some sort of patio, this chapter includes a guide to renovating and extending an existing patio.

The flagstones for this patio are being installed over a four-inch-thick concrete slab. The stones are set in a bed of mortar. After a few days, the joints will be grouted with fresh mortar.

PREPARING THE SITE

Proper site preparation is essential to the success of a patio. The process begins with building a stable, well-drained foundation. When the paving of a patio cracks, settles, heaves out of place, or experiences other structural failures, the cause almost always can be traced directly back to a poor foundation.

Getting Ready

In the design process you've already determined the size, shape, and location of your new patio, the type of paving material and edging to be installed, and the need for any new retaining walls or steps. This information is part of the basis for preparing the site. In addition, you will need to evaluate the site itself for slope, drainage characteristics, and any particular requirements, such as utility lines to be buried or a floor level to be matched.

Site preparation typically involves determining the depth of the patio foundation, laying out the perimeter of the patio, grading the site, providing for drainage, installing a gravel subbase, and building the edging. The following instructions take you through that process. They are for an attached patio measuring 12 by 15 feet; however, the process is basically the same for every type of paving material and any size patio, attached or unattached. As you read these guidelines, note any information you'll need to obtain about your site or patio design before you begin construction—information such as the drainage patterns of the yard or the thickness of the paving material. These instructions will also help you to develop a list of tools and materials you'll need, including rental tools.

Calculating the Depth of the Base

Calculate how deep the patio base must be to bring its paved surface level with the ground. Making the patio level with the ground is the easiest installation method for a do-it-yourselfer. It also prevents people from tripping over the edge and makes mowing and edging any adjacent lawns easier. In some cases there may be a compelling reason for building a raised patio, such as the need to match an existing floor level or reduce the amount of excavation into a hillside. In such cases you would have to build a raised curb, or perhaps a fairly high retaining wall, along the downslope edges of the patio.

Every patio, no matter what its paving, rests on a 4- to 8-inch-deep subbase of crushed rock or compacted pea gravel (class 5 gravel). The exact depth of the subbase depends on how deep the ground freezes in the winter. If the ground in your region doesn't freeze during a typical

Calculating Patio Base Depths

Brick-in-Sand

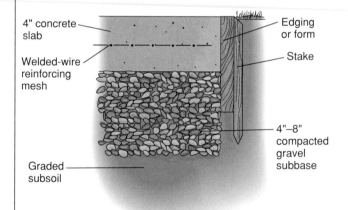

- Brick with sand joints
- 2⅔" thick
- Edging
- 2" sand setting bed
- Stake
- Graded subsoil
- 4"–8" compacted gravel subbase

Concrete Slab

- 4" concrete slab
- Welded-wire reinforcing mesh
- Graded subsoil
- Edging or form
- Stake
- 4"–8" compacted gravel subbase

Brick-in-Mortar

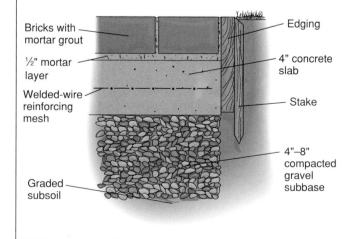

- Bricks with mortar grout
- ½" mortar layer
- Welded-wire reinforcing mesh
- Graded subsoil
- Edging
- 4" concrete slab
- Stake
- 4"–8" compacted gravel subbase

Laying Out the Site

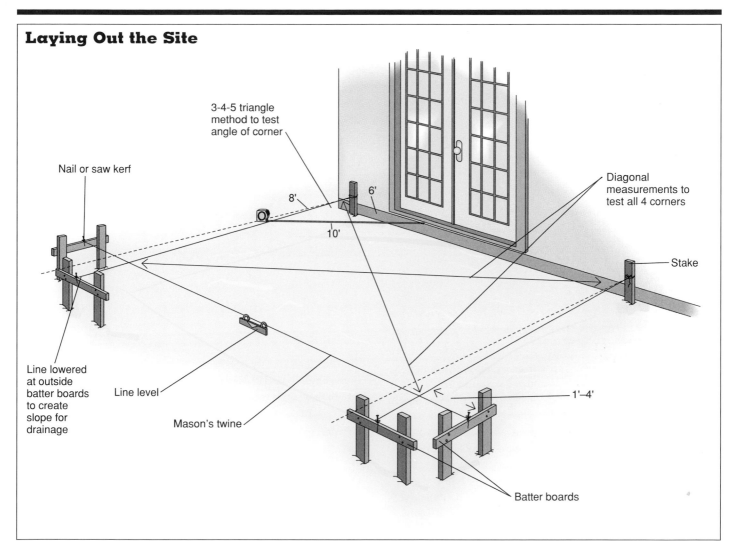

3-4-5 triangle method to test angle of corner

Nail or saw kerf

Diagonal measurements to test all 4 corners

8'

6'

10'

Stake

Line lowered at outside batter boards to create slope for drainage

Line level

Mason's twine

1'–4'

Batter boards

winter, a 4-inch-deep subbase is adequate. If the ground usually freezes, however, ask local experts how deep the frost line is. You will need to excavate to that point for the gravel layer. The gravel subbase helps to ensure adequate drainage and cushions the patio from soil movement caused by freezing and thawing.

The finished depth of the patio base depends on the depth of its gravel subbase plus the thickness of its setting bed and paving material (see illustration, opposite).

• For brick-in-sand paving, add a 2-inch-deep layer of

sand and the depth or thickness of the bricks to the depth of the gravel.

• For concrete-slab paving, add a 4-inch-thick concrete slab to the depth of the gravel.

• For brick-in-mortar paving, add a 4-inch-deep concrete slab, a ½-inch-deep layer of mortar, and the depth or thickness of the bricks to the depth of the gravel.

• For other types of paving, add the thickness of the paving material and the thickness of a 2-inch layer of sand or a 4-inch concrete slab to the depth of the gravel.

Staking the Layout

For a completely free-form and casual patio, you probably don't need to worry about an accurate layout, but for most patios it is best to start with one to make the rest of the job easier.

Using the house as a starting point, measure the patio perimeter. Drive temporary stakes into the ground at the four true corners, with the inner stakes set flush against the house. Then check for square corners using one or both of the following methods.

The first method is to measure the distance between opposite corners. If the two diagonal measurements are equal, the corners are square. If not, adjust the outer stakes until the diagonals are equal. Then double-check the length of the sides.

The second technique, the triangle method, can be used to check any given corner. It is convenient where obstacles prevent measuring the diagonals, or when the patio has a shape other than a simple rectangle. It is based on the principle of a 3-4-5 triangle, where the three sides are 3 feet, 4

Grading for Drainage

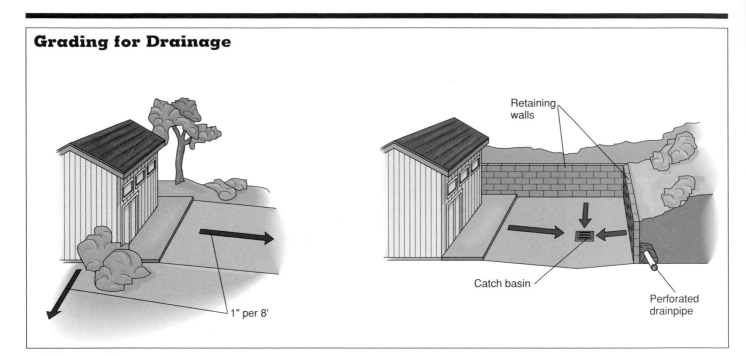

1" per 8'

Retaining walls

Catch basin

Perforated drainpipe

feet, and 5 feet long—or any multiple thereof, such as 6-8-10 or 9-12-15. Use the largest ratio possible on your size patio to ensure accuracy. Run mason's twine between the temporary stakes, pulling it taut. Working from the corner, measure along one line for 6 feet and mark that point. Measure out 8 feet along the second line, at a right angle to the first, and mark that point. Measure the diagonal distance between these two marks. If it is precisely 10 feet, the corner is square. If not, adjust either line until you get the correct measurement. Repeat this procedure at each corner as you go around the perimeter. The process may require considerable trial and error, so plan your time accordingly.

When all four corners are square, build two batter boards at right angles to each other behind each corner, setting them 1 to 4 feet back from the temporary corner stakes. For each batter board, first

drive a pair of 2×4 stakes into the ground or identify a fence, tree, or other structure to which you can nail a crosspiece. Next, using a water level or a long straightedge and carpenter's level, mark each stake (or fence) where it is level with the finished surface of the patio; if any of the marks would be below ground, raise them all an equal distance so they are all above ground, and record that distance for future reference. Then, to ensure that water will not pool next to the house, at the edge of the patio to which you want the runoff to flow, lower the marks 1 inch for every 8 feet of distance from the high edge of the patio. If this step is done correctly, the outer corners will be lower than the corners next to the house.

Next complete the batter boards by nailing on the crosspieces with the top of each crosspiece aligned with the leveling marks on the stakes.

Then set nails or saw notches in the batter board crosspieces where they align with the patio's actual corners. Stretch mason's twine between the nails or notches. Pull it taut and tie it at each batter board. After all four lines are in place, measure the diagonals to check for square corners. If done correctly, these lines will cross precisely over the temporary corner stakes. Remove the original stakes and twine. The new string lines now represent the edges of the finished patio; their intersections indicate the corners.

If any of the patio edges will be curved, establish layout lines directly on the ground using a garden hose or other long, flexible guide that will hold its shape. You can experiment with different arrangements for free-form curves. For formal curves, locate the center point of the arc on the ground, drive a stake at that point, and tie one end of a long string to it.

Measure out along the string the length of the arc's radius and, holding a stick against that point, stretch the string taut and swing an arc, scratching the stick along the ground to mark the curve.

Excavating and Grading

No matter how simple your design or how flat your lot, building a patio requires some grading. (*Grade* refers to the finished level of the ground; *grading* means excavating or filling soil to a desired level.) If nothing else, the patio surface must slope away from the house to permit runoff. Consider yourself fortunate if you can limit the grading to making this slope and still get the patio design you want. You will save time and money.

However, adding a patio to an existing yard, even one that has no serious grading problems, means you alter the existing grade. That grade

A Grid for Checking Excavation Depth

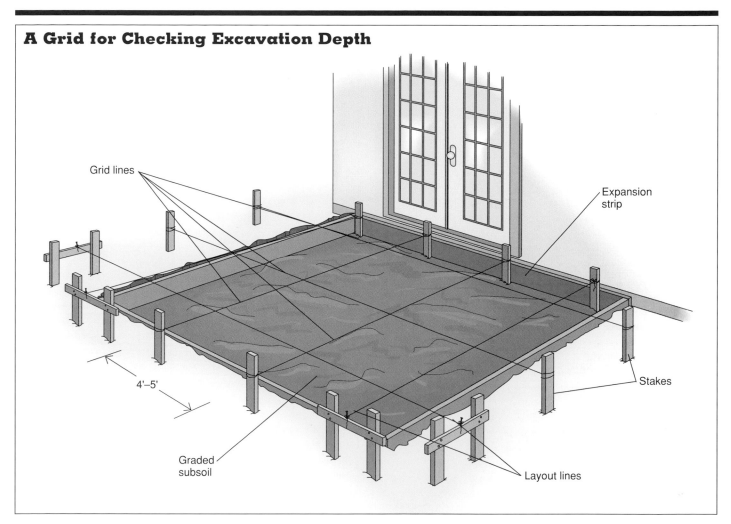

Grid lines

Expansion strip

Stakes

4'–5'

Graded subsoil

Layout lines

must be adjusted to adapt to the patio. You are stepping into especially complex situations if your yard has existing grading problems or unstable soil, or is steeply sloped, hilly, or heavily contoured for drainage. The same is true if your patio design means you must make major alterations to the existing grading. Are you confident you have the skills needed to make this adaptation? Not only is the physical work extremely hard, but the water runoff consequences are enormous—to you and to your neighbors. In addition, your community may have legal restrictions or requirements governing grad-

ing. Many communities, for example, require that you hire an engineer if you are going to make major changes to existing grading or build a retaining wall over 36 inches high. Trees, especially mature trees, are vulnerable too. They suffer when you change grading and pave over their roots. If you face any of these situations, hire a landscaping professional (see page 39) to plan and execute any new grading. The grief, sweat, and disappointment you save yourself make the expense well worthwhile.

Simple grading, however, such as the runoff pitch for a patio surface, a low retaining wall to control a slope, or a set

of steps to join two patio levels, can be done by the do-it-yourselfer. Remember, controlling drainage and providing a flat subbase are the main goals of grading.

Grading for a Patio Surface

Grade the area to be paved, using the strings as a guide, so it routes water away from the house. To excavate, first mark the perimeter of the patio on the ground by sprinkling flour or powdered chalk directly under the string lines. Where lines are more than a few inches above the ground, check the accuracy of the chalk lines

with a plumb bob; hold its string lightly against the layout line.

To guide you in keeping the bottom of the excavation uniformly sloped over the entire patio area, stretch a grid of secondary string lines. Attach them to stakes driven around the patio perimeter at equal intervals, 4 to 5 feet apart; be sure they are at the same level as your layout lines. By measuring down from the strings in this grid, you will be able to check the level of the ground within 2 or 3 feet of any other point.

Next remove sod and excavate and grade the soil within the patio area marked off by

The most effective way to tame a steep slope is with a series of low retaining walls. They create planting beds and eliminate the need for an overbearing and heavily engineered wall.

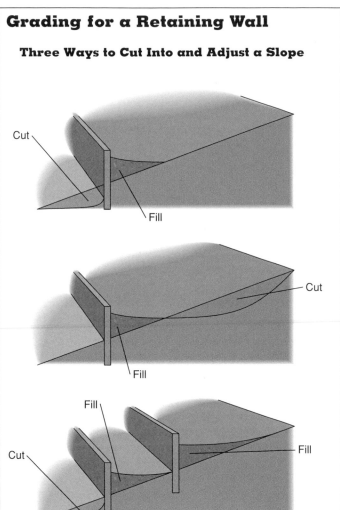

the lines. You can do this by hand if the base isn't too deep, but it is more accurate and much easier to do with a small backhoe or dump loader available from tool rental agencies. Before renting, make sure that the machine will fit through any side gates or other restricted access to the patio site. Ask the rental personnel for operating instructions.

You may need to remove the string lines temporarily while you excavate, especially if you use power equipment. Dig down to the proper depth, periodically reattaching the lines to check. This step does not have to be perfect, as the base materials will correct small irregularities, but be as accurate as possible. Try not to overdig. Your goal is a reason-ably flat surface of undisturbed soil that slopes in the direction of desired drainage. Where low areas need to be filled, add extra soil so it will settle to the desired grade when compacted.

After excavating, wet down the exposed subsoil until it is uniformly moist. Pack it into a firm surface with a power compactor, also available from a tool rental agency. Do not try to tamp by hand—you cannot produce sufficient compaction for a base of this size.

Grading for a Low Retaining Wall

When you cut into a slope, you must build a retaining wall, and then backfill with gravel.

Several ways to do this are illustrated on the opposite page. The wall can be built with many materials, including dry-stacked stone, boulders, wood, brick, mortared concrete blocks, poured concrete, or interlocking retaining-wall blocks. Note that the retaining wall rests on uncut, undisturbed ground or on concrete footings regardless of the method or material used. It never rests on fill. Grading techniques will vary with local conditions. If the ground is stable, you may make a vertical cut. If not, you will have to remove a great deal of soil to keep the hillside from caving in. Consult a professional about any conditions you are not sure about, or if the cut will be higher than 3 feet.

When excavating for a retaining wall, take drainage into consideration. Drainage is important because the wall will fail if water builds up behind it. That means you must provide a way to channel water away from the wall as well as off the patio. The solidity of the wall complicates the situation, but the task can still be done. After the wall is built,

Common Retaining Walls

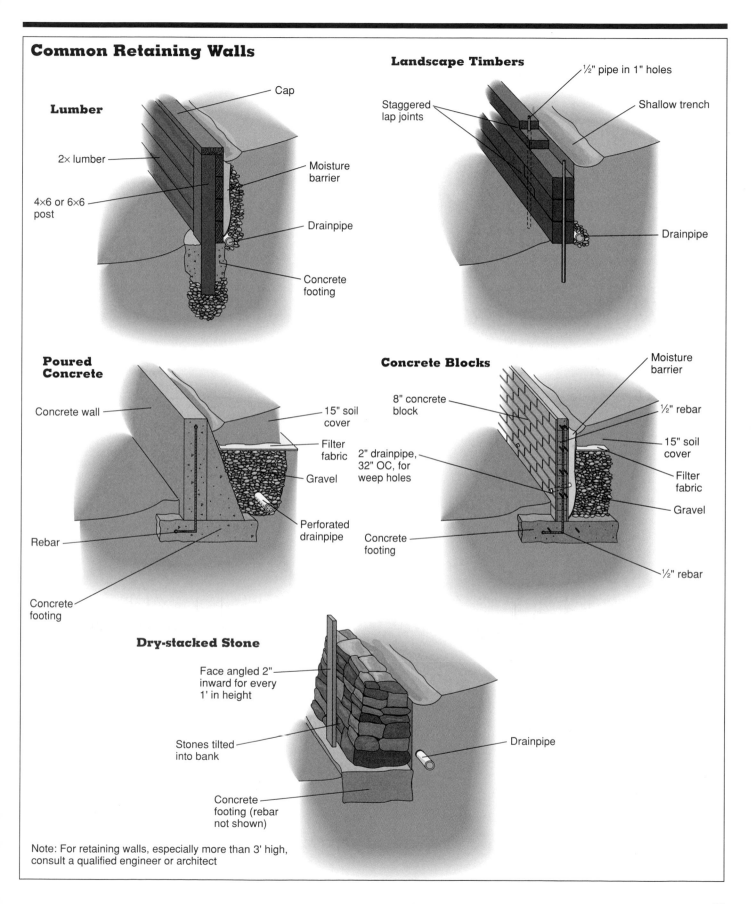

Lumber

- Cap
- 2× lumber
- 4×6 or 6×6 post
- Moisture barrier
- Drainpipe
- Concrete footing

Landscape Timbers

- ½" pipe in 1" holes
- Staggered lap joints
- Shallow trench
- Drainpipe

Poured Concrete

- Concrete wall
- 15" soil cover
- Filter fabric
- Gravel
- Perforated drainpipe
- Rebar
- Concrete footing

Concrete Blocks

- 8" concrete block
- 2" drainpipe, 32" OC, for weep holes
- Concrete footing
- Moisture barrier
- ½" rebar
- 15" soil cover
- Filter fabric
- Gravel
- ½" rebar

Dry-stacked Stone

- Face angled 2" inward for every 1' in height
- Stones tilted into bank
- Drainpipe
- Concrete footing (rebar not shown)

Note: For retaining walls, especially more than 3' high, consult a qualified engineer or architect

Grading for Steps

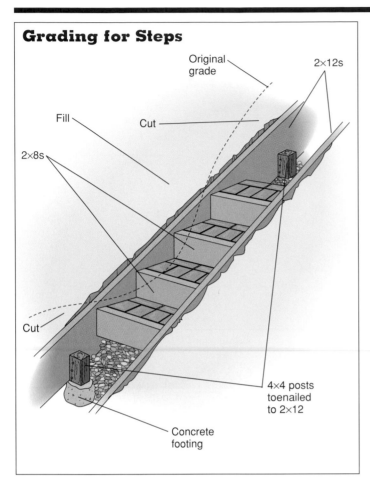

Original grade

Fill

Cut

2×8s

Cut

2×12s

4×4 posts toenailed to 2×12

Concrete footing

create a shallow ditch behind the top of the wall to catch and divert surface water. You can control subsurface water in two ways. The first is to bury 4-inch perforated polyvinyl chloride (PVC) drainage pipe in the gravel backfill along the base of the wall, excavating accordingly. Slope the pipe ¼ inch per foot toward one or both ends of the wall. The second method is to build weep holes (gaps between paving units or short lengths of pipe that pierce the wall) into the wall along its base.

Grading for Steps

When excavating for steps, use the following general guidelines. Steps work much the same way as retaining walls. They also can be built with the same materials. The flight of steps itself should be at least 3 feet wide; a 4-foot to 6-foot width is much more comfortable and attractive. All the steps in the flight must have the same dimensions. In addition, each tread should have a ⅛-inch per 1-foot drainage pitch toward its front edge. Ideally, the front edge of each tread also overhangs its riser by ¾ inch to 1 inch to allow water to drip down onto the next step. This is not possible with all materials, however.

Providing Surface Drainage

The correct drainage pitch and a proper gravel foundation usually provide adequate drainage for a patio. However, subsurface water can build up under its surface in regions where rainfall is frequent and heavy, where spring snowmelt gets trapped, where the natural water table is high, where a patio sits in clay soil, or where a steep hill or slope causes heavy runoff. Such a buildup wreaks havoc with patio paving. If there is any possibility this can happen, give your patio an underground drainage system.

Drainage systems take three forms: subsurface drainage pipes, perimeter channels, or a catch basin. They must all drain to a low place away from the patio and house, but not into your neighbor's yard, onto public property, or, in many communities, the street gutter. If you do not have a suitable drainage outlet on your property, you will have to build a dry well.

Subsurface Drainage Pipes

This method is for patios with the paving material laid in sand, where water can seep directly below the patio. Depending on the size of the patio, dig a narrow trench along the edges and/or down

the center of the patio area. The depth of this trench varies by climate; check with local experts for the correct depth for your area. Slope the trench ⅛ inch per foot and place 2 inches of 1-inch drain rock along the bottom. Place PVC or acrylonitrile-butadiene-styrene (ABS) drainage pipe, connected and with the holes down, in the trenches. If the outlet is farther than 10 feet from the patio, use solid rather than perforated pipe for the distance beyond 10 feet. After the pipes are in place, backfill the trenches with drain rock or gravel, place a drain fabric or other filtering material over the gravel, and cover with topsoil.

Perimeter Channel

If the patio has a solid surface of concrete or mortared paving materials, form and pour a narrow concrete channel, 3 to 4 inches deep, around the patio perimeter, close to the edges, or lay concrete drain tiles along the patio edges. The channel should be narrow enough that it can be bridged with one piece of paving material. Put a thin layer of gravel in the bottom of the channel and lay lengths of perforated drainage pipe on top of it, holes down. Then backfill around the pipe with more gravel. As you lay the paving materials over this pipe, leave the joints between the pieces ungrouted (open) so water can run across the patio to the edges and drain into the channel.

Draining a Patio Surface

Subsurface Drainpipe

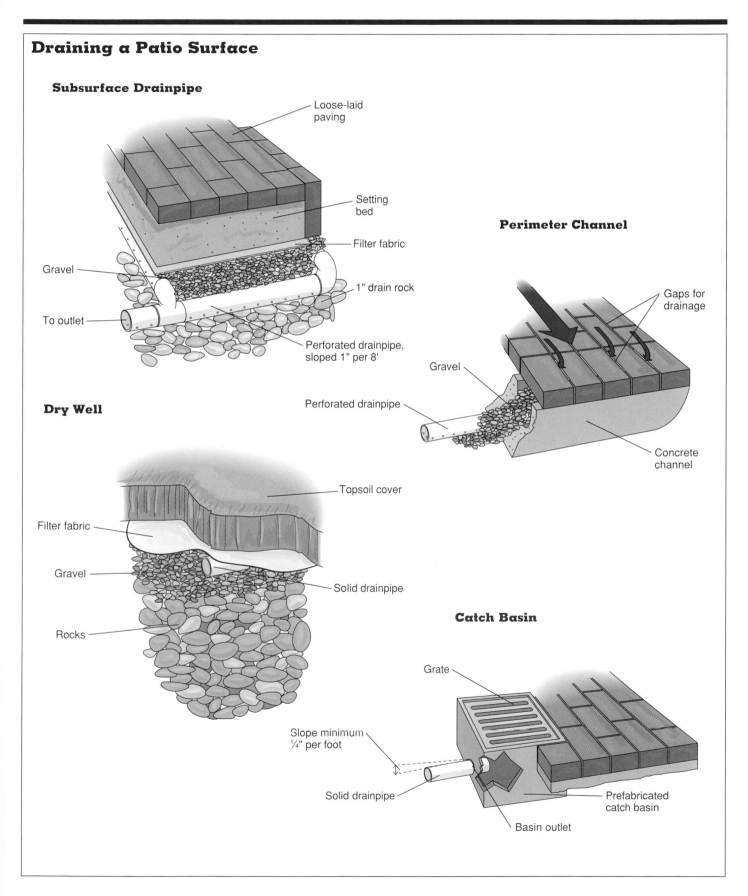

Loose-laid paving

Setting bed

Filter fabric

Gravel

1" drain rock

To outlet

Perforated drainpipe, sloped 1" per 8'

Perimeter Channel

Gaps for drainage

Gravel

Perforated drainpipe

Concrete channel

Dry Well

Topsoil cover

Filter fabric

Gravel

Solid drainpipe

Rocks

Catch Basin

Grate

Slope minimum ¼" per foot

Solid drainpipe

Basin outlet

Prefabricated catch basin

Catch Basin

A catch basin works especially well for draining water off a patio surrounded by a retaining wall. Determine where you want the patio's lowest point to be; its finished surface will slope toward it. Dig a hole under this point and line it with ready-mixed concrete or a plastic catch basin, available at building-supply outlets. Dig a trench from the side hole of the catch basin to where you want the water dumped—a dry well, a drain field, or a storm sewer if your community permits that. Place lengths of solid drainage pipe in this trench and top the catch basin with a grate. Water draining from the patio into the basin will run out the pipe to the dumping field provided.

Dry Well

Any of these methods may require a dry well. To build one, dig a 2- to 4-foot-wide hole somewhat away from the patio. Ideally, this hole is at least 3 feet deep, but it must be above the water table. Direct the runoff pipes from the patio into the dry well. Fill the dry well with coarse gravel, top it with a waterproof material such as heavy roofing paper, and cover with topsoil and sod. Water collected in the dry well will seep into the ground naturally.

Laying the Foundation

The composition of a patio foundation is basically the same for all patios. Once you have a properly graded and firmly packed soil base that establishes the drainage

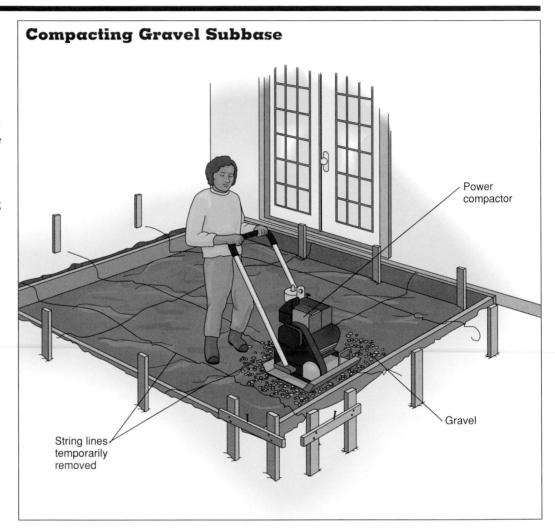

Compacting Gravel Subbase

Power compactor

Gravel

String lines temporarily removed

pitch, the next step is to place the gravel.

Installing the Gravel

Place gravel on top of the soil base in 4-inch-deep layers. Spread the first layer evenly with a rake. Wet it down and pack it into a uniform surface with a power compactor. Repeat this process until the gravel subbase is the correct depth and has a solid surface capable of supporting the setting bed and paving. Tamp down the gravel with the compactor a final time. If you plan to lay the paving material in sand, you may want to cover

the gravel layer with a filter fabric to keep particles of sand or other fine material from clogging the gravel and inhibiting drainage.

How Much Gravel to Buy?

Use the formula for calculating how much concrete to order (see page 48) to determine how many cubic yards of gravel you need for the subbase. Gravel is sold by the ton or by the cubic yard. Ask the dealer to make the conversion from tons to cubic yards, or vice versa. Have the gravel unloaded as close to the patio site as possible, and have lots

of helpers to transport it in wheelbarrows.

Installing Patio Edgings

Except for poured concrete patios without a permanent edging, install edging materials after the gravel subbase is in place. The edging will guide placement of the final paving materials, especially those that are loose laid. For a poured concrete patio that will not have a permanent edging, or for a foundation slab, install the form boards at this point (see page 75). Use the illustration opposite as a guide to installing the patio edging.

Common Edging Installations

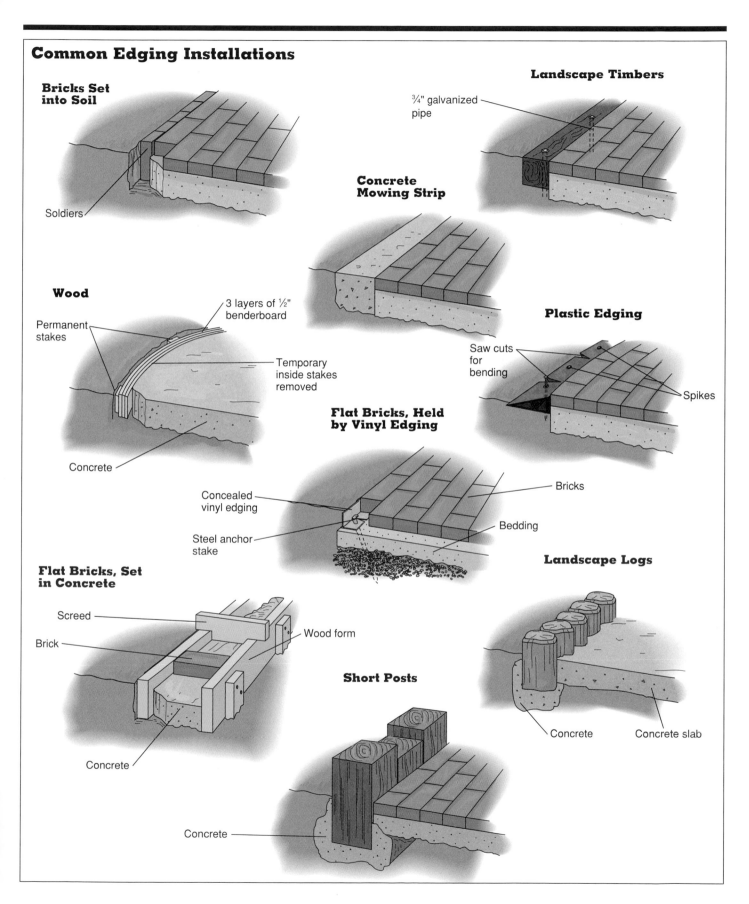

Bricks Set into Soil

Soldiers

Landscape Timbers

¾" galvanized pipe

Concrete Mowing Strip

Wood

Permanent stakes

3 layers of ½" benderboard

Temporary inside stakes removed

Concrete

Plastic Edging

Saw cuts for bending

Spikes

Flat Bricks, Held by Vinyl Edging

Concealed vinyl edging

Steel anchor stake

Bricks

Bedding

Flat Bricks, Set in Concrete

Screed

Brick

Wood form

Concrete

Short Posts

Concrete

Landscape Logs

Concrete

Concrete slab

BUILDING A BRICK-IN-SAND PATIO

For the do-it-yourselfer, a brick-in-sand patio is the easiest to install. It is attractive, reasonably durable, and serviceable. It is also quite inexpensive, and you can further reduce costs by using interlocking concrete pavers; the installation techniques are the same as for bricks.

Before You Start

There are several advantages to choosing brick-in-sand for your patio. Along with attractiveness and easy installation, a brick-in-sand patio offers the do-it-yourselfer another tremendous advantage: Because you don't have to worry about mortar setting up, you can lay as little or as much brick at a given time as you wish. You also can use the patio as soon as it is finished, because you don't have to wait for mortar to dry or cure.

There are very few specialized tools and even fewer technical skills required to install this type of patio. Besides measuring, counting, leveling, and shoveling, you will have to be able to cut bricks, which you can quickly learn to do if you have the right tools. You will also need to operate a power compactor, which is a hilarious experience you won't want to miss. The store personnel where you rent the machine will give you the few simple instructions for operating it. As with any project, planning the job carefully before you begin, so you have the right equipment and know what to expect, will give you all of the confidence you need for a successful installation.

Having the Right Tools

You probably already have most of the tools needed to lay brick: a steel tape measure, framing square, 2-foot-long carpenter's level, hammer, mallet, mason's twine, line level, wheelbarrow, and safety goggles. In addition, you need the following professional bricklaying tools, which you can borrow, rent, or buy, to make the job easier.

• A mason's level, at least 4 feet long, for checking level over large areas.

• A brickset or broad-bladed cold chisel for cutting and trimming bricks.

• A mason's hammer for trimming the rough edges of cut bricks.

• Brick tongs for carrying several bricks at a time.

• A screed for leveling the sand.

• A power compactor, to pack the gravel, sand, and brick paving.

Cutting Bricks

Inevitably, you must cut some bricks to make your pattern fit within the patio space. Always wear safety goggles to protect your eyes from flying chips and grit.

If you have just a few cuts to make, use a brickset or broad-bladed cold chisel, beveled edge facing the waste piece, to score a cutting line on all four sides. Do this by tapping the handle gently with a hammer. Then lay the brick flat on the sand, face side up, and place the tool on the scored line, its beveled edge again facing the waste piece. Strike the handle with a sharp blow of the hammer. The brick

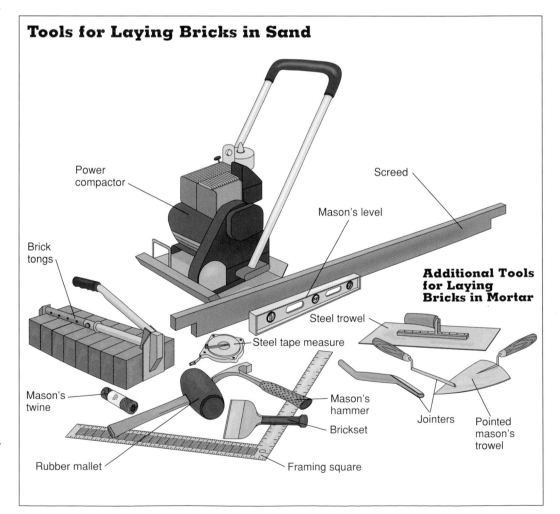

Tools for Laying Bricks in Sand

Power compactor

Screed

Mason's level

Brick tongs

Additional Tools for Laying Bricks in Mortar

Steel trowel

Steel tape measure

Mason's hammer

Jointers

Pointed mason's trowel

Mason's twine

Brickset

Rubber mallet

Framing square

Cutting Bricks

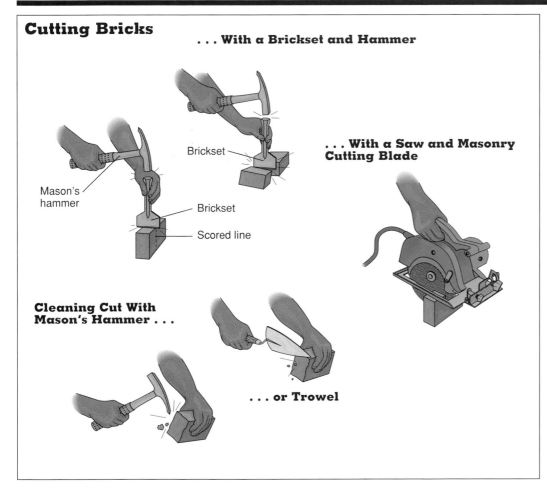

. . . With a Brickset and Hammer

Mason's hammer

Brickset

Brickset

Scored line

. . . With a Saw and Masonry Cutting Blade

Cleaning Cut With Mason's Hammer . . .

. . . or Trowel

will break into two pieces along the scored line. Trim the rough edges with the brickset or a mason's hammer.

If the job involves many cuts, wait until the end and make them all at one time to ensure speed and accuracy. Consider renting a hydraulic brick cutter. This large, stationary tool uses pressure to score and cleanly cut bricks, although you still have to trim them somewhat.

If you need to make a lot of angle cuts or need very smooth cuts, rent a diamond-bladed tile saw.

Install the Edging

The first step in laying a brick-in-sand patio, after the site is prepared, is to install the edging to hold the sand and bricks firmly in place. Install edging after the subbase is laid and compacted but before

Cross Section of Brick-in-Sand Patio

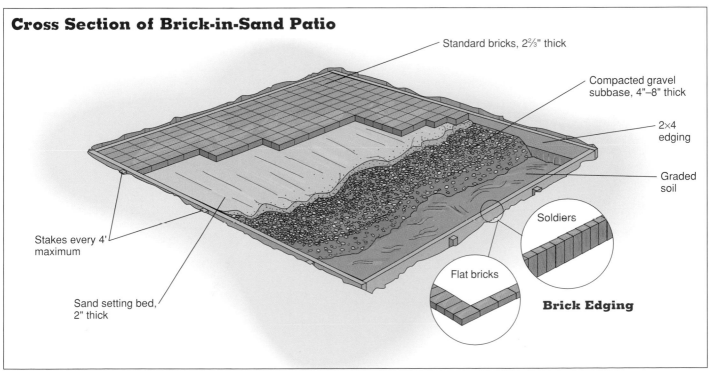

Standard bricks, 2⅔" thick

Compacted gravel subbase, 4"–8" thick

2×4 edging

Graded soil

Soldiers

Flat bricks

Brick Edging

Stakes every 4' maximum

Sand setting bed, 2" thick

Leveling Sand Setting Bed

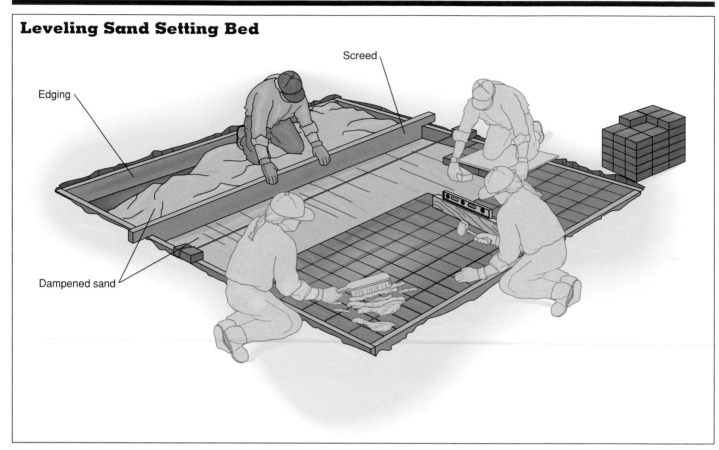

Edging

Screed

Dampened sand

Setting Bricks

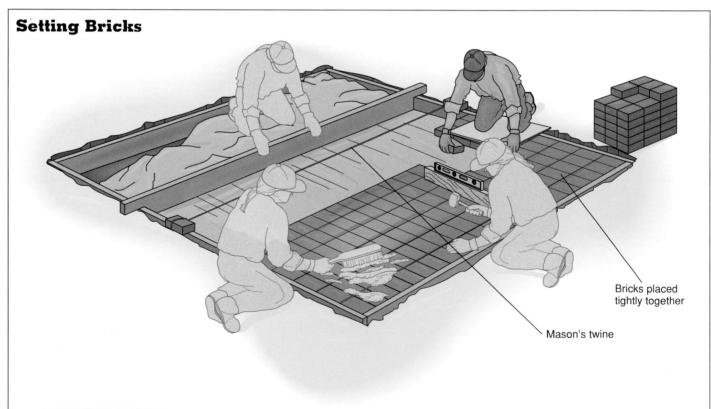

Bricks placed
tightly together

Mason's twine

Seating Bricks

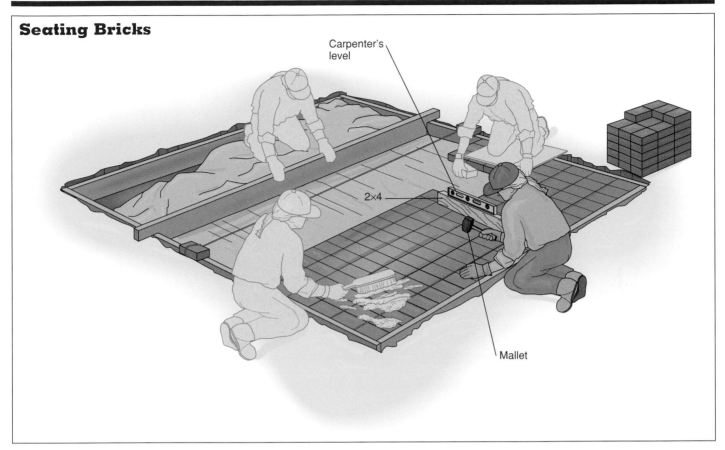

Carpenter's level

2×4

Mallet

laying the setting bed and paving. Dimensional lumber, a concealed concrete footing, poured concrete, and bricks set into the soil all provide the stable edging this kind of patio needs. See pages 56 and 68 for a discussion of the different types and how they are installed.

If possible, adjust the over-all patio dimensions, and build the edgings accordingly, so very few end bricks will need to be cut to fit within the edgings. However, unless you are experienced or very lucky, the bricks will not be perfectly aligned for your first installation. Also, it is easy enough to make up for shortfalls as you go by slightly increasing the gaps between bricks. So do not spend a lot of time fussing over the dimensions.

Making the Setting Bed

A brick-in-sand setting bed consists of a 2-inch-deep layer of sand spread on top of the gravel subbase. Use the formula for estimating how much concrete to order (see page 48) to determine how many cubic yards of sand you need to make this bed.

Wet down the gravel sub-base and cover it with sand. Using a shovel, spread the sand as evenly as possible over the gravel. Then screed or level it into a uniform, 2-inch-deep layer over the entire surface. This is the most important step in constructing this type of patio.

Make a screed from a straight 2×4 a bit longer than the width of the patio. On

each end, make a cutout 1½ inches deep (from the bottom edge) and long enough so the screed will ride on the patio edging and/or temporary guides. Working 3-foot-wide sections at a time, pull the screed in a sawing motion as you level the sand. Tamp the sand with a power compactor until the surface is firm. Add more sand if needed, and screed and tamp until you have a firm, 2-inch-deep layer. If you're using a weed block-ing fabric to control weeds, now is the time to install it over the sand.

Laying the Bricks

Dampen the sand, then start laying the bricks in one corner, butting them tightly together

in your chosen pattern. Don't slide the bricks into place—this shifts the sand. Instead, place each brick straight down into the sand and press it firmly into place with a ham-mer handle or mallet. Lay one course at a time, using mason's twine to keep the courses straight. Frequently as you work, use a carpenter's level on a straight 2×4 to check for level. If you want the patio surface to be sloped for drainage, cut the 2×4 to a tapered shape to represent the degree of slope (1 inch per 8 feet of length) so the level will read accurately. If a brick is too low, lift it and tamp a little damp sand under its low side to level it. If it is too high, lift it and gently scrape out some of the sand and tamp to level it.

Spreading Sand Fill

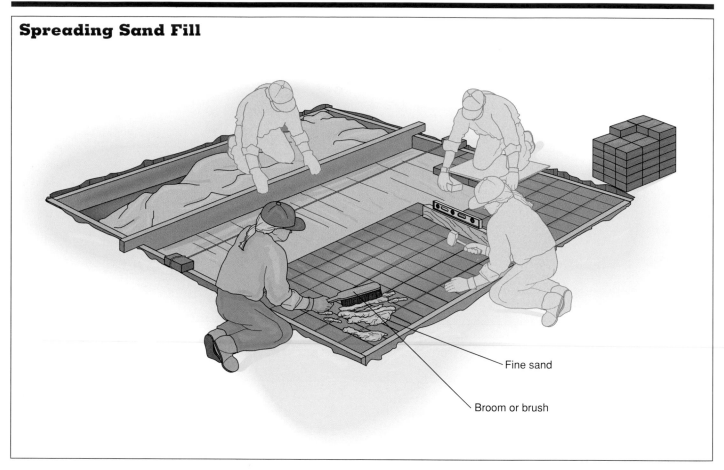

Fine sand

Broom or brush

Adding the Sand Fill

When all of the bricks are laid, cover the entire surface with a thin layer of fine sand. Work it around with a broom until the joints are filled. Spray the surface with a fine stream of water to compact the sand, being careful not to flood the joints. Repeat the sanding and spraying procedure until all the joints are packed full of sand. You can create an even more stable installation by using the power compactor to pack the bricks after filling the joints with sand. Place pieces of plywood over the bricks and run the compactor over them a few times, just as you did to tamp the gravel base and setting bed.

Making Dry-Mortar Joints

Brick-in-sand patios can be given mortar joints. The process is the same as for sand-filled joints, only dry mortar is used in place of sand. Lay the bricks with ½-inch gaps between them. Sprinkle a dry mix of 1 part cement and 4 parts sand over the patio surface. Use a stiff-bristled brush to sweep the mortar into the joints. When they are full, tamp the mortar into place with a ½-inch-thick piece of wood. Add more dry mix if needed to completely fill the joints, sweeping it into the joints. Wet the surface using a fine spray so you don't splash mortar out of the joints; don't let the water pool. Keep the mortar damp for two to three hours. When it is firm, tool the joints with a mason's jointer. After a few more hours, scrub off any mortar on the bricks.

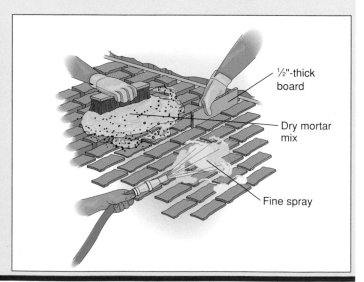

½"-thick board

Dry mortar mix

Fine spray

BUILDING A POURED CONCRETE PATIO

Although more involved than setting bricks in sand, building a concrete patio is relatively inexpensive and is within the abilities of most do-it-yourselfers. There are dozens of interesting ways to create an attractive finished surface, or you can use the basic concrete slab as a foundation for other paving materials.

Preparing for the Pour

Concrete gives you a stable patio surface that lasts a lifetime if it is correctly installed. However, fresh concrete is a cumbersome material. It is heavy and requires you to work fast. Once the pour starts, you can't stop until the section is complete—struck-off, floated, edged, grooved, and troweled. That means you need two or more helpers for a patio measuring 12 by 15 feet, more if the patio is larger or you have to transport concrete to the work site in wheelbarrows. It also means that

you must be prepared: The forms have to be in place, you need the right tools on hand, and the concrete order must be accurate.

There is no advantage to mixing concrete yourself for a project as large as a patio. As dramatic as the concrete pour itself is, it is relatively unimportant to the final outcome of the project when compared with what must go on before and after the pour. In effect, all concrete work is divided into two phases—before the pour and after the pour—so you shouldn't focus on the pour itself any more than you have to. Handling bulk materials

and mixing concrete is misplaced effort.

The Necessary Tools

Besides a wheelbarrow, line level, square-sided shovel, and steel tape measure, you probably don't have the specialized tools necessary to give concrete a professional finish. You need these finishing tools to do a credible job.

• A pointed mason's trowel to smooth, cut, scrape, and chip concrete.

• A screed or strike-off board to level the wet concrete.

• A bull float or a darby to smooth out the wet concrete. A bull float is a large, long-handled float used on large surfaces. A darby is a hand-held wood tool used to float small surfaces.

• A wood float to give concrete a slightly coarse finish.

• A steel trowel to give concrete a smooth, glassy finish.

• An edging tool to form smooth edges.

• A metal grooving trowel or jointer to cut expansion or control joints.

You also need protective clothing. These items include thick work gloves to protect your skin from the caustic concrete, and heavy rubber work boots. Don't wear any clothes you can't afford to throw away when the job is done; standard cleanup should take care of most stains, but you don't want to take any chances.

Building the Formwork

Concrete is heavy and must be contained in well-braced forms. Make the forms and stakes with 2×4 lumber. Remember, 2×4 lumber is actually 3½ inches wide, whereas the concrete slab is actually a true 4 inches thick. To make up for this difference in depth, place ½ inch of backfill under the lumber so its top edge is flush with the ground, and concrete cannot seep under it.

Concrete Tools

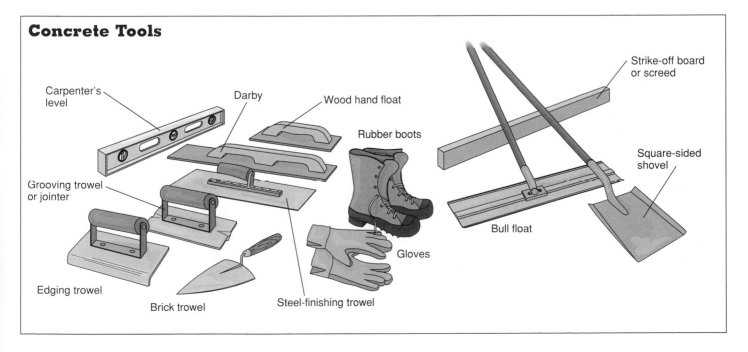

Carpenter's level

Darby

Wood hand float

Rubber boots

Strike-off board or screed

Grooving trowel or jointer

Square-sided shovel

Bull float

Edging trowel

Gloves

Brick trowel

Steel-finishing trowel

There are two types of forms: temporary, which are removed after the concrete has cured, and permanent, which are incorporated into the patio surface.

Temporary Forms

Place the form boards around the patio perimeter, butting them end-to-end. The inner side of the boards forms the slab's finished edge. Along the backside of the 2×4s, drive the stakes into the ground at 4-foot intervals and at every joint. Drive them slightly below the top edges of the boards. Secure them by driving double-headed nails through the stakes into the forms. Just before the pour, dampen the forms with an oil or release agent to make them easier to remove.

Permanent Forms

Permanent forms become part of the patio's decorative treatment. Make them with heart redwood, cedar, or cypress that has been given a coat of clear wood sealer, or with pressure-treated lumber, which requires no preparation except coating any cut ends with preservative.

Join the boards at the corners with neat butt or miter joints. Drive the stakes 1 inch below the ground. Secure them by driving 16-penny (16d) hot-dipped galvanized (HDG) nails through the stakes into the boards. Also drive 16d HDG nails horizontally through the boards, at midheight, every 16 inches around the perimeter. These nails help anchor the boards to the poured concrete. Cover the

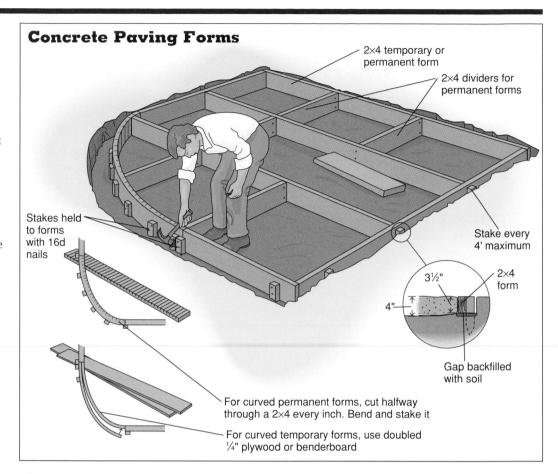

Concrete Paving Forms

2×4 temporary or permanent form

2×4 dividers for permanent forms

Stakes held to forms with 16d nails

Stake every 4' maximum

3½"

4"

2×4 form

Gap backfilled with soil

For curved permanent forms, cut halfway through a 2×4 every inch. Bend and stake it

For curved temporary forms, use doubled ¼" plywood or benderboard

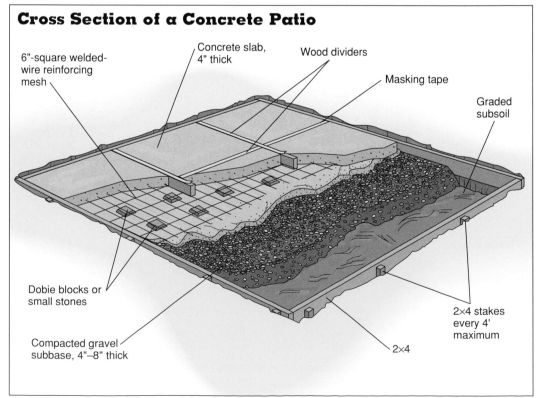

Cross Section of a Concrete Patio

6"-square welded-wire reinforcing mesh

Concrete slab, 4" thick

Wood dividers

Masking tape

Graded subsoil

Dobie blocks or small stones

Compacted gravel subbase, 4"–8" thick

2×4

2×4 stakes every 4' maximum

top edges of the form with masking tape to prevent staining and other damage during the pour.

As you build both types of forms, check them frequently with a level to make sure the proper grade and slope are maintained. And with both types of forms, install a band of flexible concrete joint foam where the patio butts the house.

Making the Setting Bed

Once the formwork is built, dampen the compacted gravel subbase. Lay 6-inch-square welded-wire reinforcing mesh (called 6-6-10-10 reinforcing mesh) over the gravel. At frequent and regular intervals, lift the mesh and slip small stones or pieces of brick under it so it is held 1 to 2 inches above the gravel. If you install the wire in sections, overlap the sections by one square. Be careful when working with the mesh; it must be cut with a hacksaw or bolt cutters, and should be straightened as you unroll it, or it might spring back into a coil shape without warning.

Adding Divider Strips

If the patio is large, install divider strips at this time. They replace control or expansion joints as well as give the patio a decorative finish. They also give you the advantage of breaking the patio surface into sections that can be poured and finished one or two at a time.

Place these divider strips at a maximum of 10-foot - intervals in both directions. Because they will remain in the concrete, make them of 2×4 heart redwood, cedar, or cypress or pressure-treated lumber. Give redwood, cedar, or cypress dividers a coat of clear wood sealer before installing them; pressure-treated dividers need no chemical treatment.

No matter what wood you use, join the intersecting strips with neat butt joints and secure by toenailing. Reinforce the divider joints with stakes driven into the ground outside the forms. Drive 16d HDG nails through these interior dividers to help anchor the concrete after it is poured (the same as with the permanent forms—except drive them alternately from opposite sides of the boards). Cover the top edges of the dividers with masking tape to prevent them from being stained or damaged during the pour.

Ordering Concrete

If you plan to use ready-mixed concrete, see page 48 for estimating instructions. If you live where the ground freezes in the winter, be sure to specify that you want air-entrained concrete. When ordering, specify a 5-sack mix with ¾-inch aggregate (the number of sacks of portland cement per yard of concrete, and the maximum size of the gravel). Indicate that you are pouring a patio. If the concrete truck cannot reach the patio (chutes are 16 feet long), you should also arrange for a pump truck—either through the ready-mix dealer or on your own. Tell the ready-mix company which pumping service you are using, so they can coordinate their delivery. Also, verify that the hose on the pump truck can accommodate ¾-inch aggregate, which requires a 4-inch-diameter hose. If not, order ⅜-inch pea gravel instead, which can be pumped through a 3-inch-diameter hose.

Mixing Concrete Yourself

Mixing your own concrete is worthwhile only if you are paving a small area, or if you can pour and finish the concrete in workable sections that are no more than 3 feet square. If you plan to mix the concrete yourself, you could buy sacks of dry ready-mixed concrete, but it would be more economical to purchase bulk ingredients. Whichever you choose, rent a portable cement mixer; proper mixing is essential so the cement paste coats

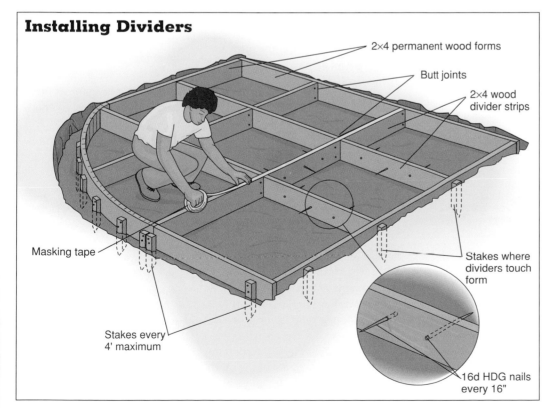

Installing Dividers

2×4 permanent wood forms

Butt joints

2×4 wood divider strips

Masking tape

Stakes where dividers touch form

Stakes every 4' maximum

16d HDG nails every 16"

Mixing Concrete

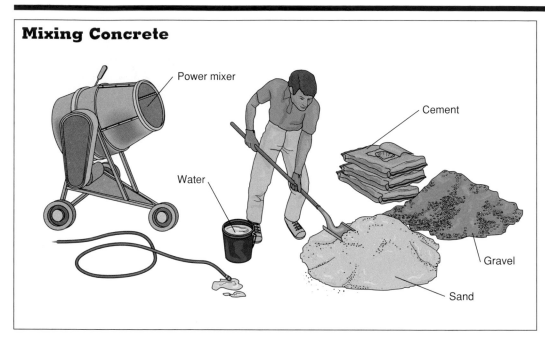

Power mixer

Water

Cement

Gravel

Sand

Testing Moisture Content of Sand

Damp sand falls apart when squeezed in your hand

Wet sand forms a ball but leaves no noticeable moisture in your hand

Very wet sand forms a ball and leaves noticeable moisture in your hand

every particle of sand and coarse aggregate in the mix. Simply stirring ingredients together will not do. A portable cement mixer mixes ⅔ cubic yard at a time.

If you plan to use dry ready-mixed concrete, an 80-pound bag yields ⅔ cubic foot of concrete. Figure the patio's cubic feet using the formula given on page 48, multiply by 0.66, and add 10 percent.

Successful concrete comes from the proper combination of cement, sand, aggregate, and water. A standard mixture for patios and walkways is 1 part cement, 2¼ parts sand, 3 parts coarse aggregate, and ½ part water. You also need to add an air-entraining agent if you live in a region with freezing weather.

The amount of water you actually use depends on how much water the sand contains. Because sand is always sold wet, make a test batch in the mixer. Start by estimating the moisture content of the sand: Pick up a handful and squeeze

it. If it tends to crumble, it is merely damp, and you need more than ½ part water. If it compacts smoothly without visible water in your hand, it is wet or average and you need ½ part water. If it forms a ball and leaves your hand soaked, it is very wet and you need less than ½ part water.

Based on your estimate of the sand's moisture content, mix a trial batch of concrete. Dump a small amount onto the ground and examine it for stiffness and workability, or "slump." *Slump* refers to the number of inches a 12-inch-high pile of concrete slumps when fresh. A 1-inch slump is a very stiff mix, a 10-inch slump very soupy. For residential purposes, a 4-inch slump is average. The ideal mixture is plastic, almost smooth and creamy; with light troweling, all the spaces between the pieces of aggregate fill with sand and cement. If the trial batch is not right, adjust the ingredients for another trial batch and combine in the mixer for at least one minute. Check again, and keep adjusting until you get the right mix.

Pouring the Concrete

Before you pour the concrete, give the forms a final check for trueness to grade and proper slope. Then wet down the forms and the gravel so they do not absorb water from the concrete.

Begin the pour in a corner at one end of the patio and work across and forward in the space. Pour uniformly to the full depth of the form and as close as possible to the final

A Well-Coordinated Concrete Pour

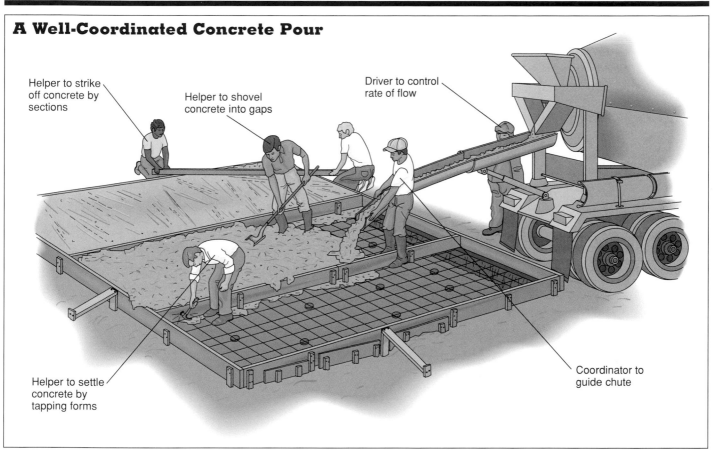

Helper to strike off concrete by sections

Helper to shovel concrete into gaps

Driver to control rate of flow

Helper to settle concrete by tapping forms

Coordinator to guide chute

Spreading Concrete

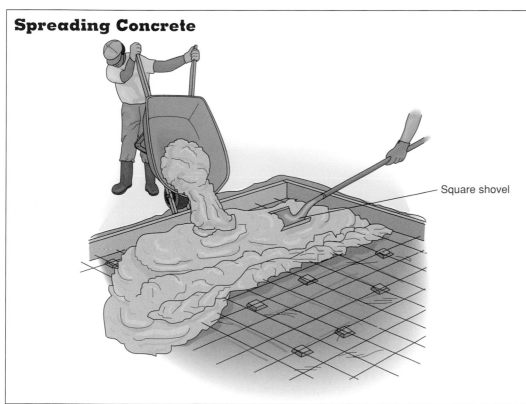

Square shovel

position. Immediately begin spreading the concrete with the square-sided shovel. Work it up against the forms and tamp it into the corners and down into the reinforcing mesh. Spread it only enough to compact it firmly and eliminate voids. Do not overwork it—this brings excess water and inert silt to the surface. The next batch goes up against the previous one.

Leveling and Smoothing Concrete

As soon as the concrete has been spread and compacted (batch by batch, if you wish), strike-off and float the slab. Both steps must be done before water oozes out and collects on the surface.

Striking Off Concrete

Screed

Floating Concrete

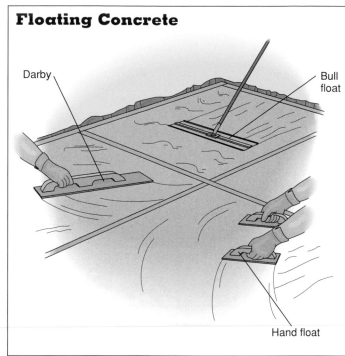

Darby

Bull float

Hand float

Striking-off

It takes two people to strike-off a large slab, one at each end of the screed. The screed can be a wood straightedge or a straight 2×4 that is 12 to 18 inches longer than the width of the slab. Slide it slowly along the tops of the forms in a sawing motion, covering a 36-inch-long section in one pass. Go back over the section a second time to remove any remaining bumps. Fill low spots with shovelfuls of concrete and screed level. If the slab has dividers, one person can strike-off, doing one section at a time.

Floating

This step immediately follows the strike-off. It levels ridges and fills voids left by the screed and helps compact the concrete. It also embeds the coarse aggregate slightly below the surface. Use either a darby (for small surfaces) or a

bull float (for larger surfaces) for this job.

• For smaller surfaces, hold the darby flat against the concrete and work it back and forth in a sawing motion. When the surface is level, tilt the darby slightly and go over the surface again, working in one direction. Although a wood darby works fine, rent or borrow a magnesium float if you can; it slides more evenly over the concrete without the slight drag of a wood one.

• For larger surfaces, push the bull float away from you, the front end of its blade raised slightly so it doesn't gouge the concrete. Then pull it back with the blade flat on the surface.

Immediately after floating, use a mason's trowel to cut the concrete away from the forms to a depth of 1 inch. Then let the concrete begin to set up before continuing with the finishing steps. This waiting period can be as long as

several hours, depending on the weather.

Finishing Concrete

Concrete is ready for finishing when its watery sheen is gone and foot pressure leaves no more than a ¼-inch-deep indentation. Waiting for the concrete to reach this stage is the only way to get a durable surface. When the slab reaches the desirable point, continue with the finishing steps in this order: edging, jointing, hand-floating, and troweling.

Edging

This first finishing step produces a neat, rounded edge that resists chipping. It also compacts and hardens the concrete surface next to the forms. Hold the edger flat on the surface next to the forms and run it back and forth to make a shallow, smooth edge. Raise its front edge slightly

when moving it forward, and its back edge when moving backward, so you don't gouge the concrete.

Jointing

Immediately after edging, cut or groove control joints in the slab no more than 10 feet apart. This is the most important finishing step because it provides a place for the concrete to crack as it expands and contracts with the weather. If the slab has wood dividers, you've already provided these joints, and you can skip this step. If you don't have dividers, mark the joint locations on the concrete surface with a chalk line, striving for a pleasing appearance. With a 1×6 as a straightedge, and a wooden pad to kneel on, cut the joints with a handheld metal grooving trowel or jointer or a circular saw fit with an abrasive blade; guide the tool along the straightedge for a straight line.

• When cutting with a grooving trowel, use one with a sharp bit deep enough to cut a 1-inch joint in the slab. Push it down into the concrete and slide it forward. Apply pressure at the back of the groover to keep it from gouging the concrete. When the cut is complete, turn the groover around and go back over the joint to create a smooth finish.

• When cutting with a circular saw, make saw joints when the surface is hard enough not to be torn or damaged by the blade. Normally, this is 4 to 12 hours after the concrete hardens. Cut the joints 1 inch deep and finish them by running the edger over them.

Hand-Floating

Hand-floating removes imperfections, compacts the concrete surface, and prepares it to receive a finish. Use a wood hand float to produce the skid-resistant finish recommended for a patio. Hold it flat against the surface and move it in a sweeping arc with a slight sawing motion. If you want a slightly rougher texture for the patio, float the surface a second time instead of troweling (the next step). Floating usually removes the marks left by the edger and groover. If you want these marks for decorative purposes, rerun the edger and groover over the edges and joints after this step.

Troweling

Troweling produces a smooth, hard surface considered undesirable for patios. However, it makes a good surface on

which to apply textured finishes. Using a steel trowel, place the blade flat on the surface and move it in a sweeping arc, each pass overlapping the previous pass by half its width. If this step does not produce as smooth a texture as desired, do a second and even a third troweling. Leave the forms in place for at least 24 hours, and preferably 5 days, after this last step, but begin curing immediately.

Curing

Curing keeps the concrete moist and warm so it hardens properly. When done correctly, this step gives the concrete slab maximum strength and durability. There are three ways to keep it moist.

• Use an oscillating lawn sprinkler or soaking hoses. Apply the water continuously and uniformly so the slab does not partially dry out; wet/dry cycles cause cracks.

Edging and Cutting Joints

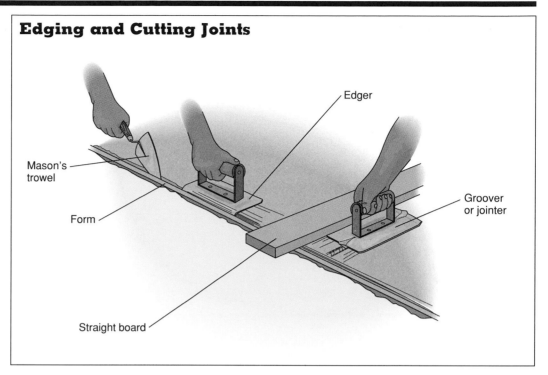

Mason's trowel

Form

Straight board

Edger

Groover or jointer

Finishing Concrete

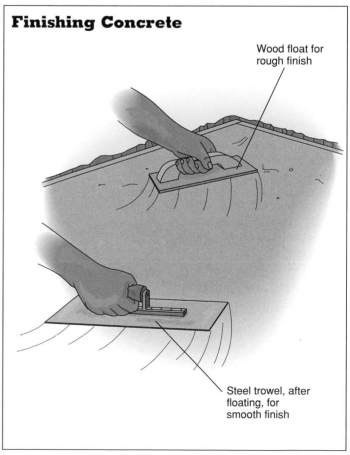

Wood float for rough finish

Steel trowel, after floating, for smooth finish

Curing Concrete

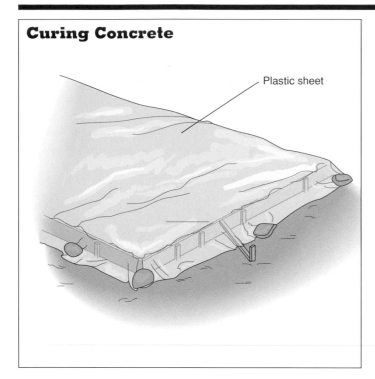

Plastic sheet

• Cover the slab with burlap or straw and keep the material uniformly wet. Covering the burlap or straw with plastic sheeting helps.

• Cover the slab with plastic sheeting, wet burlap, waterproof paper, or curing compounds that prevent moisture loss. These materials must be laid flat, thoroughly sealed at the joints, and anchored carefully along the edges.

There also are colored curing compounds that provide an easy and convenient way to cure concrete (see opposite).

Continue the curing process for five days in warm weather (70° F or higher), for seven days in cool weather (50° to 70° F). Add three days to the curing time for every day the temperature falls below 50° F. Do not allow the temperature of the concrete to fall below 50° F during this curing period.

When moist curing is complete, remove the coverings

or stop sprinkling and let the slab dry out naturally. This is a long, slow process that takes up to several months. Do not walk on the concrete during the first 24 hours after curing.

Decorative Finishes

Applying a decorative surface treatment gives concrete a pleasing texture and improves its traction.

Exposed Aggregate

This is the most popular concrete finish. It is slightly rugged and naturally colorful. This finish is achieved by exposing the aggregate mixed into the concrete or by seeding additional aggregate into the surface.

• Exposing the internal aggregate. Construct the slab through the first floating stage. Be careful not to overfloat, pushing the coarse aggregate too deep into the

Seeded Aggregate Finish

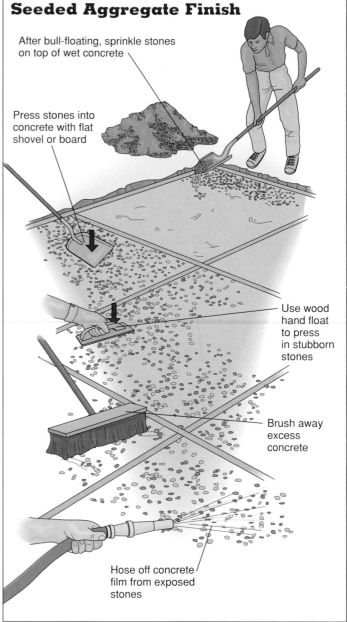

After bull-floating, sprinkle stones on top of wet concrete

Press stones into concrete with flat shovel or board

Use wood hand float to press in stubborn stones

Brush away excess concrete

Hose off concrete film from exposed stones

slab. When the watery sheen disappears and the slab bears your weight on knee pads without indentation, brush away the top layer of concrete with a stiff nylon brush or broom until you have just exposed the aggregate. Clear away the concrete debris. Spray the surface with a curing agent (available at concrete suppliers), cover it with

a plastic sheet, and let it cure for 24 hours. Then repeat the brooming process, accompanied by a fine spray of water, until about half the surface of the large stones is exposed.

• Seeding aggregate. If you plan to seed aggregate into the slab, build the forms ½ inch lower than the desired final surface to allow for its thickness. Construct the slab

Coloring Concrete

Concrete is naturally gray and dull, but it doesn't have to be that way. You can color it in any of six ways—one-course, two-course, dry shake, colored curing compounds, chemical stains, and paint. The first three methods give the most satisfactory results because the colors become integral to the concrete and are subtle and attractive. They soften and subdue the gray rather than just mask it.

One-Course Method

In this method, pigment is mixed with the concrete before it is poured, to produce a uniform coloration throughout the body. The pigment is pure mineral oxide or a synthetic iron-oxide colorant prepared for use in concrete. Both types of pigment yield satisfactory results. Buy them from building materials suppliers. Make sure the pigment is insoluble in water, free of soluble salts and acids, and sunfast. For subtle, pastel colors, use 1½ pounds of pigment to every bag of cement. For stronger color, add 7 pounds of pigment to every bag of cement. The colors range from white, cream, and buff to green, pink, rose, and brown.

Two-Course Method

Similar to the one-course method, this technique uses a base course of standard concrete and a top coat of colored mortar (cement, sand, water, and color pigment). The pigments are the same as for the one-course method. The surface of the base course is left rough enough to provide a good bond for the top coat. After the base coat stiffens slightly and the surface water disappears, mix the pigment into the mortar and apply in a ½-inch- to 1-inch-thick layer. Apply a commercial bonding agent or a cement grout before floating and troweling the mortar in place (see page 90).

Dry Shake Method

Powdered color consists of pigment, white portland cement, and a silica sand or fine aggregate and acts as a concrete hardener. It is available from a concrete supplier. Following the directions on the label, sprinkle about two-thirds of the powder evenly over the slab. As soon as the powder absorbs some of the moisture, thoroughly hand-float it into the surface. Immediately, shake the remaining powder evenly over the surface, allow it to become absorbed, and hand-float into the slab.

Colored Curing Compounds

Curing compounds are spray-on solutions that are applied over fresh concrete to help it harden properly. Most are clear but some have colored additives. Inquire about the availability of colored curing compounds at your concrete supplier. Like paint, this is only a surface treatment and may wear off.

Chemical Stains

These stains, which must be applied by a licensed contractor, are made by blending together metallic salts, water, and acid solutions. They enhance concrete with a wide variety of striking colors in mottled and drifted color patterns. The contractor spreads the solution on a clean, dry concrete slab and allows it to stand for a specified period of time as it color-etches the surface. Chemical stains can be used in combination with the other coloring methods described above to make interesting patterns.

Paint

Paint is the least desirable way to color any masonry surface. It simply does not stand up well to heavy traffic and rough weather conditions, and it requires constant upkeep. Use it only if absolutely necessary. Before painting, the surface must be cured for 28 days to 6 months and completely cleaned (see page 81). Use a primer and paint specifically formulated for use on concrete surfaces.

1" thick layer of colored concrete

Dry shake method

Paint or chemical stain

Texturing Concrete

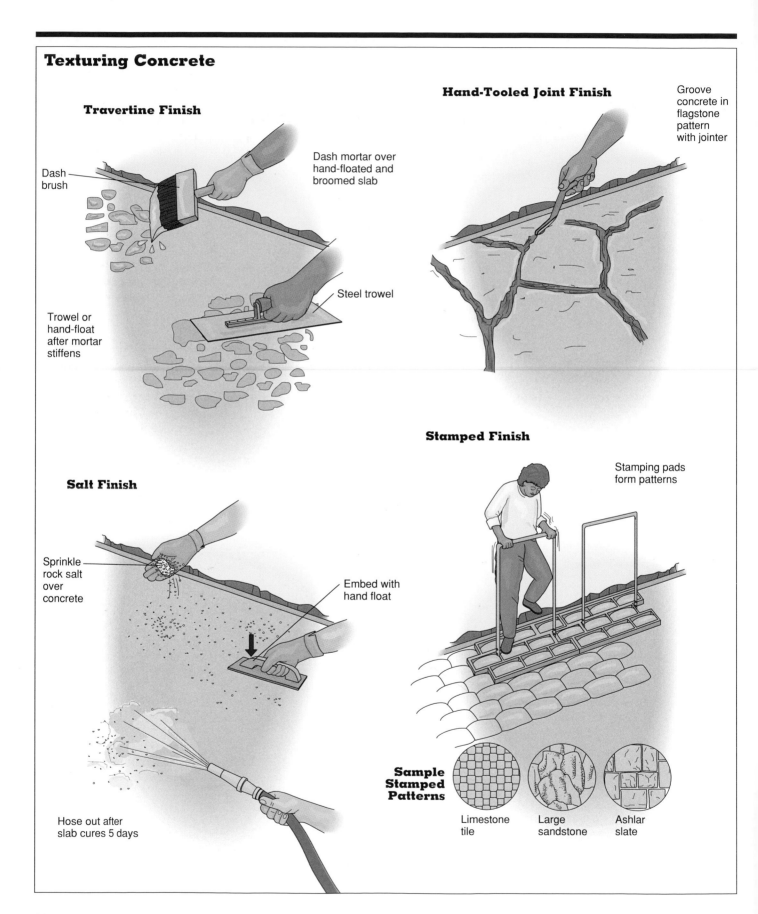

Travertine Finish

Dash brush

Dash mortar over hand-floated and broomed slab

Steel trowel

Trowel or hand-float after mortar stiffens

Hand-Tooled Joint Finish

Groove concrete in flagstone pattern with jointer

Salt Finish

Sprinkle rock salt over concrete

Embed with hand float

Hose out after slab cures 5 days

Stamped Finish

Stamping pads form patterns

Sample Stamped Patterns

Limestone tile

Large sandstone

Ashlar slate

through the first floating stage. Spread the aggregate over the surface in an even layer. Using a wood hand float, a darby, or a straight board, tap the aggregate into the concrete. Then use a bull float or hand float to embed the aggregate in the concrete until the mortar just surrounds all the pebbles. This surface aggregate should not intermix with the base aggregate. Make sure the surface remains flat, then expose the seeded aggregate in the same way you expose internal aggregate.

Troweled Finish

This is a swirled pattern made with a trowel. It gives a patio an interesting texture and good traction. Build the slab through the first hand-floated stage. Texture the surface by holding a trowel flat, pressing on it, and moving it in a swirling motion. Make different patterns with a series of uniform arcs or twists.

Broomed Finish

This attractive, nonslip texture is created by pulling damp brooms across freshly floated or troweled concrete. Apply the texture in straight, curved, or wavy lines. For the best results, use a broom specifically made for texturing concrete.

Travertine Finish

This attractive surface resembles travertine marble. It requires a two-step procedure. After the slab has been edged, sweep it with a broom to create a surface that will bond with a finish or mortar coat, which is made by mixing white portland cement with sand, color pigment, and water. Throw the mortar onto the slab with a dash brush. When the slab can support you on knee boards, use a steel trowel to flatten the ridges and spread the mortar, leaving voids in the low areas. This finish is not recommended for regions with freezing weather.

Rock Salt Finish

This is a slightly pitted, roughened surface created by rolling rock salt into the concrete. It creates an interesting texture and provides excellent traction. Scatter the salt over the surface after it has been hand-floated, troweled, or broomed. Then, with a hand float, roll or press the grains into the concrete until only their tops remain exposed. A water cure won't work with this finish; instead, cure it for five days under plastic sheeting or waterproof paper. Then wash and brush the surface to dissolve the salt. Continue curing as needed. This finish is not recommended for areas with freezing weather.

Semismooth Finish

This is a slightly rough or coarse texture produced by hand-floating the concrete with a wood float and stopping there. The wood float drags, creating the texture. It is a good texture for a nonskid surface.

Smooth Finish

Create this surface by troweling the concrete two or three times with a steel trowel. This tool compacts the concrete, producing a hard, smooth surface. This is not an ideal surface for a patio, but it does make a good base for texturing techniques such as brooming and salting.

Stamped-Pattern Finish

Concrete often is made to resemble other paving materials by incising it with stamping pads, which come in patterns that resemble brick, cobblestone, flagstone, cut stone, slate, pavers, and exotic materials such as wood boardwalk. After the slab has been floated, place the pads on the concrete, carefully aligning them with one another and pressing them into position. Then step from one pad to the next, using your weight to cut the pattern 1 inch deep into the concrete. After stamping, use a mason's jointer to clean up the joints. Stamped concrete is usually colored (see page 83).

Hand-Tooled Finish

With a concave jointer or a piece of bent ½-inch to ¾-inch copper pipe, cut patterns to resemble joints around flagstones. After the slab is floated, score the pattern into the surface. Score a second time after the slab has been hand-floated. Hand-tooled concrete is usually colored too (see page 83).

To divide a concrete patio with stone or brick strips, place shallow forms, in a grid pattern, on the surface of the patio before the concrete is poured. After the concrete hardens, remove the forms and set the stone or brick into the voids with fresh mortar.

UILDING A BRICK-IN-MORTAR PATIO

There is a long tradition for this type of patio. It is permanent and attractive and combines the benefits of a concrete slab with the warmth and elegance of brick. The grouted joints create a strong pattern, setting this type of patio apart from brick-in-sand installations.

Providing a Foundation

Laying bricks in wet mortar creates a handsome and stable patio surface that is especially desirable in rainy climates. You need a concrete slab as a base. It can be a new slab or an existing one that is in good condition or has been repaired. Make sure the slab is thoroughly clean and roughen the surface to promote a solid bond between the old and new surfaces. If you are building a new slab, don't think about a decorative finish. Float it with a wood float to give it a roughened surface, then cure. Wait two weeks after the initial curing before laying the bricks.

Setting the Bricks

First, following the instructions on page 56, install the brick edging around the slab perimeter. The top should extend above the slab a distance equal to one brick thickness plus ½ inch. This type of installation lends itself to half-bricks, which are face bricks half as thick as conventional ones. When the edging is finished, you are ready to lay the bricks.

Wet the bricks and the existing concrete slab thoroughly so they will not pull water out of the mortar. Use a dry ready-mix or make your own mortar by mixing 1 part cement with 4 parts wet sand. Mix only the amount you can use in 1 hour. Plan to work one 3-foot-square section at a time.

Spread the mortar in the working section and strike-off to a ½-inch depth. Using mason's twine to align the bricks, lay them in the desired pattern, leaving ½-inch open joints between them. As you set each brick in place, tap it gently with a rubber mallet to seat it in the mortar. Check frequently for level as you work. Wait at least 24 hours before finishing the joints.

Grouting the Joints

Add ½ part hydrated lime to the mortar mix to improve workability. Pack the mortar into the joints between the bricks with a pointed mason's trowel, keeping it off the bricks as much as possible; immediately clean up any spills with a moist rag. Let the joints harden for about 30 minutes, then finish the joints by lightly tooling them with a mason's jointer. Keep the mortar wet for 24 hours by covering with a plastic sheet. Stay off the brick surface for at least three more days.

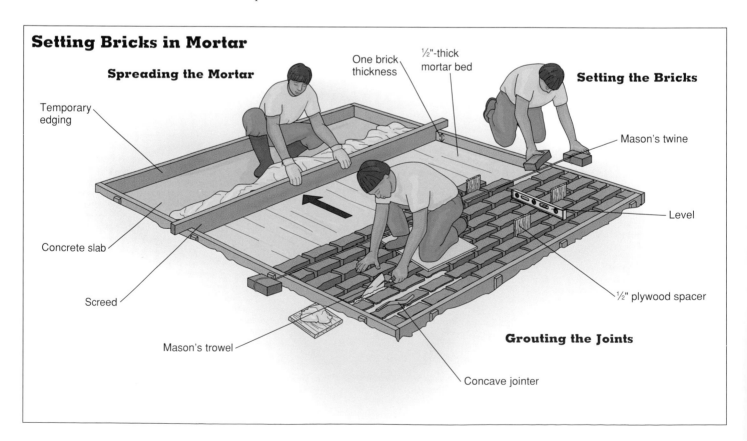

Setting Bricks in Mortar

Spreading the Mortar

Temporary edging

Concrete slab

Screed

Mason's trowel

One brick thickness

½"-thick mortar bed

Setting the Bricks

Mason's twine

Level

½" plywood spacer

Grouting the Joints

Concave jointer

RENOVATING AN EXISTING PATIO

You don't need to rip out an existing patio just because it shows some wear and tear or is too small to meet your current needs—not unless it is so badly damaged it can't be repaired. That is seldom the case. Instead, clean and repair the existing surface and use it as the beginning of a new, larger patio.

Evaluating the Existing Patio

Look over your existing patio carefully. If you like its location and it is solid and sound, it is useable and worth saving. Solid and sound means it doesn't have large or deep cracks, has not sunk or started to break up, and needs only cleaning and minor repairs. Use it as the core or centerpiece of a new, larger patio, or use it as the setting bed for a completely new patio surface. If it has deteriorated badly, however, it probably does not have a solid base. Remove it and start over.

Breaking Up an Existing Patio

Dismantling a brick-in-sand patio is tedious but simple. Break up one corner brick with a hammer. Then, using a crowbar, lift out the bricks and set them aside. Then dig a new base and build an entirely new patio, or turn the space into lawn or garden beds.

Demolishing a concrete slab is another story. It is hard work. Look in the Yellow Pages under "Concrete Breaking, Cutting, and Sawing" for contractors who specialize in this work. A contractor saves you a lot of backbreaking labor and hauls away the heavy debris as well.

If you want to do the work yourself, you need a variety of special tools; rent them if necessary.

• Crowbars and sledgehammers for breaking and lifting concrete.

• Machines for cutting concrete, especially if it is thicker than 4 inches or has steel reinforcement. These include a pneumatic or electric jackhammer and a concrete saw.

• Personal safety gear, such as safety goggles, ear protectors or earplugs, leather gloves, and sturdy boots.

Using Hand Tools

Wielding a sledgehammer or crowbar takes strong arms, determination, and a lot of sweat equity, but it works well if the slab is no more than 4 inches thick. Wear safety goggles to protect your eyes from flying chips. The secret to success is to use the hammer just enough to create a few cracks, then use a long crowbar to lift out small sections. Concrete breaks more easily when it is pried upward than when it is pounded downward. The failsafe method is a combination of both motions.

Working With a Jackhammer

There are two types of jackhammers, pneumatic and electric. Pneumatic jackhammers

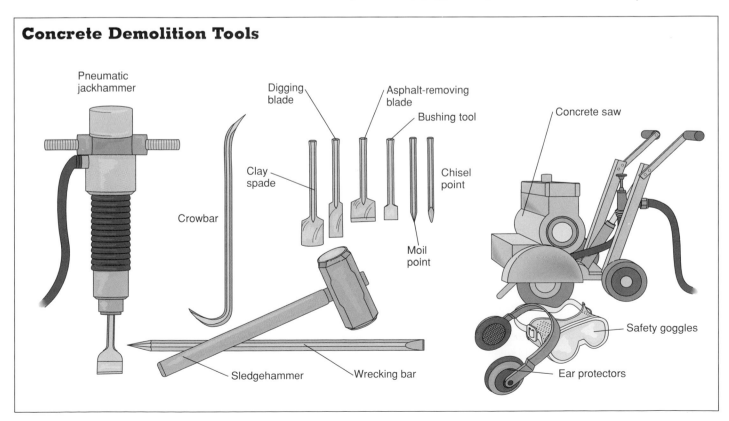

Concrete Demolition Tools

Pneumatic jackhammer

Digging blade

Asphalt-removing blade

Bushing tool

Concrete saw

Clay spade

Crowbar

Chisel point

Moil point

Sledgehammer

Wrecking bar

Safety goggles

Ear protectors

are heavy tools that operate on air supplied by a gasoline- or diesel-powered compressor. They are sized by the amount of air the compressor supplies, which is stated in cubic feet per minute (cfm). The hammer weighs about the same as its cfm rating. A 30-pound hammer is good for slabs up to 3 inches thick; a 60-pound hammer for slabs up to 4 inches thick (the standard depth for patios). Electric jackhammers are smaller, quieter, and more convenient to use because they don't require a separate air compressor. They're less powerful than pneumatic hammers because they run on 110-volt household current, but are adequate for most residential demolition work. Although 30-pound electric jackhammers are available, use a 60-pounder on patio slabs from 2 to 4 inches thick.

Let the jackhammer do the work. Balance it with your hands and arms and don't lean on it. It works best if you break off the concrete in 3- to 5-inch-wide chunks. Be sure to wear safety goggles and ear protection.

Cutting With a Concrete Saw

Use a concrete saw when you want to remove only a section of concrete, leaving the rest of the slab intact. You can also use it to score the slab, which you can then break up with a sledgehammer. Run by a gasoline-powered engine, this saw uses either a masonry cut-off blade or a diamond-edged blade. Usually, you have to buy the masonry cutoff blade outright. You can rent a

diamond-edged blade for an additional fee. It is more cost-effective to rent the diamond-edged blade if you need to cut more than 40 linear feet of concrete.

Get instructions for operating the saw from the rental agency. Typically, the procedure is to start the motor, position the blade over the cutting line, and slowly lower it through the concrete. Move it forward, but don't push hard—the engine propels the saw forward; forcing it can cause the blade to break. For a clean finished edge, cut all the way through the slab. For an unfinished edge, make a ½-inch-deep scoring cut, and break up the slab with a sledgehammer. Obviously, a scoring cut is easier and faster to make.

Covering an Existing Patio

Don't use an existing patio as the base for a new patio surface unless it is sound, solid, and reasonably level. Whether brick or concrete, an unstable surface does not make a good base for a new patio. The patio face must be roughened and cleaned for a proper bond between the old and new concrete. To thoroughly roughen the surface, rent a scarifier, grinder, or sandblaster. Follow all instructions and recommended safety precautions. You may want to hire professionals to do this dusty work. Clean the surface by spraying it with a garden hose. This rinse removes any masonry and metal grit left behind by the roughening process.

The cleaned, roughened existing patio surface becomes

the setting bed for the new surface.

• Pouring concrete over an existing concrete slab. Build new forms and follow the instructions for pouring a concrete slab (page 78). Before you pour the new concrete, you can ensure bonding by drilling holes around the edges of the existing slab (don't go below the concrete to dirt). Cement reinforcing rods in these holes so they extend 6 inches above the slab. When the cement has hardened, slide a length of galvanized pipe over the rods and bend them toward the interior of the patio so they extend horizontally 2 inches above the old slab. Tie welded reinforcing mesh to them, place small stones under the wire to hold it up in the center, then pour the new slab.

• Paving concrete with brick. Follow the instructions for laying brick in wet mortar (page 86). Start by installing a new edging.

• Pouring concrete over brick. Make sure all the sand fill is removed from the joints. Build new forms and follow the instructions for pouring a concrete slab (page 78).

Repairing and Enlarging a Brick-in-Sand Patio

Generally, brick-in-sand patios wear very well. The bricks stay in place if the patio has a good base and proper edging. Periodically weeding the joints and refilling them with sand is the only routine maintenance required. Refilling the joints is done as for a new brick surface (page 86). The biggest problems associated with a brick

patio are moss and algaelike growths on the surface, and an occasional heaved brick.

Cleaning Brick

To remove moss, mildew, algae, and lichen, make a cleaning solution of 1 ounce laundry detergent, 3 ounces nonphosphate substitute for trisodium phosphate (TSP), 1 quart chlorine bleach, and 3 quarts water. Brush this solution onto the stained areas and let sit for five minutes, then rinse.

To remove grease, oil, and food deposits, scrub with a solution of laundry detergent and warm water, then rinse. If oil has penetrated the brick surface, saturate the area with mineral spirits or paint thinner and cover with an absorbent material, such as dry portland cement, cat litter, fuller's earth, cornmeal, or cornstarch. Let stand overnight and then sweep away. Repeat if necessary. If this does not work, make a paste of benzol and one of the above dry materials and apply to the stain. Leave in place for one hour after the benzol has evaporated. Repeat if necessary.

Remove other stains the same way you remove them from fabric. If this doesn't work, contact a ready-mix dealer or your county extension agent for directions.

Replacing Bricks

To reseat a heaved brick, dampen the sand under it and tap it back into place with a mallet. Occasionally, you need to replace cracked or broken bricks. Using a crowbar, pry up the damaged brick, whether it is standard brick

Replacing a Damaged Brick

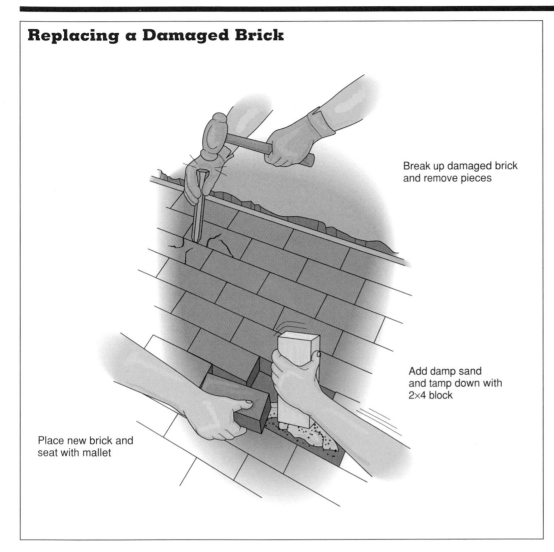

Break up damaged brick and remove pieces

Add damp sand and tamp down with 2×4 block

Place new brick and seat with mallet

or a paving brick. If it doesn't pry easily, break it up with a hammer and cold chisel. Dampen the sand under it, then set a replacement brick in its place and tap it with a mallet to seat it in the sand. When you have replaced all the defective bricks, sand-fill the joints as you would a new brick surface (page 74).

Coloring Brick

Painting is not a effective way to disguise bricks that don't match, or to change a brick color you don't like. There are two better solutions to these problems.

• If you can't find matching bricks with which to replace the damaged ones, work out a random design for the patio that uses bricks that contrast or coordinate with the original bricks. Incorporate into the new design the bricks that must be replaced. Remove and replace all the bricks needed to complete the design.

• Treat unmatched bricks, or bricks whose color bores you, with a chemical masonry stain. These stains are blended solutions of metallic salts, water, and acid, which etch and color any masonry surface. The colors can be mixed together

or diluted to produce a wide variety of subtle, mottled colors. Such treatments are most successful when applied by a licensed applicator.

If you must paint bricks, understand that the paint will not hold up well in high-traffic areas. It will have to be renewed frequently. It will also take a lot of paint, because the porous surface sucks it up like a sponge. Be sure the surface is scrupulously clean by washing it with a solution of 5 to 10 percent muriatic acid. Apply a coat of masonry primer, followed by one or two coats of a masonry paint.

Enlarging a Brick-in-Sand Patio

Fortunately, because brick is too valuable a material to waste, it is easy to enlarge a brick-in-sand patio. Use the existing patio as the center or the lead-off edge of a new, larger surface and build the additional patio around or adjacent to it. If the new surface is brick, follow the instructions for installing a brick-in-sand patio (page 70). If it is a contrasting material such as concrete, follow the instructions for installing a concrete slab (page 75). Either way, you must dig a new base. Don't worry about the existing base crumbling when exposed; if it was compacted correctly, it will stay intact. If a few stones escape, push them back into place when you lay the new gravel subbase.

Repairing and Enlarging a Concrete Patio

As durable as concrete is, years of wear and weather make occasional repairs and cleaning necessary.

Cleaning Concrete

General cleaning consists of an occasional washing with laundry detergent and water, followed by a clear water rinse. Apply the detergent solution with a stiff-bristled broom, and scrub stubborn spots with a brass or stainless steel wire brush. If this doesn't clean the surface sufficiently, try etching it with muriatic acid. Mix 1 part acid into 9 parts water in a nonmetallic container. Saturate the concrete with water, then brush the solution onto the concrete with a long-handled, stiff-bristled broom. Let stand 5 to 10 minutes and then rinse thoroughly with water. When cleaning with the acid solution, wear rubber gloves, eye protection, and old clothes, and follow all instructions on the label.

Clean away moss, mildew, algae, lichen, and oil stains the same way you clean them from brick (see page 88). Remove other stains the same way you remove them from fabric. If this doesn't work, contact a ready-mix dealer or your county extension agent for directions.

Repairing Concrete

A clean surface is the beginning point for any concrete patch job. The cleaning process includes removing any loose or deteriorated concrete, clearing away particles and dust, and roughening the surface to ensure a tight bond. Although a proper bond is achievable with either a damp or dry surface, the best bond develops if the base concrete is dry. Lightly dampen the surface only during hot weather.

For all repairs, cover the cleaned area with a commercial bonding agent or an ⅛-inch-thick layer of portland cement grout. Follow the manufacturer's directions if you use a commercial bonding agent. To make the grout, mix equal parts of portland cement and sand with water until the mixture has the consistency of thick paint.

•Repairing minor surface imperfections and wear. These flaws include dusting (the surface wears away easily),

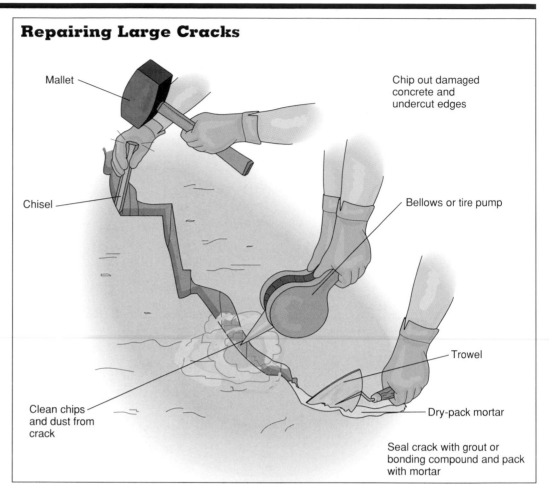

Repairing Large Cracks

Mallet

Chisel

Clean chips and dust from crack

Chip out damaged concrete and undercut edges

Bellows or tire pump

Trowel

Dry-pack mortar

Seal crack with grout or bonding compound and pack with mortar

scaling (thin layers flake off), spalling (deeper layers flake off), and crazing (fine networks of surface cracks form). Before the bonding agent or the grout dries, coat the area with a mortar made by mixing water with 1 part portland cement and 3 parts sand. Trowel smooth, feathering the edges into the existing surface, and cure (see page 81).

•Filling small holes and popouts. Repair these defects by filling them with a dry-pack mortar or a commercial patching compound. Make the dry-pack mortar by mixing 1 part portland cement and 2½ parts sand with just enough water to make a ball when molded by hand. Before the

This large crack was planted with woolly thyme (Thymus pseudolanuginosus), *an aromatic herb tough enough to tolerate foot traffic.*

Repairing Areas of Damaged Concrete

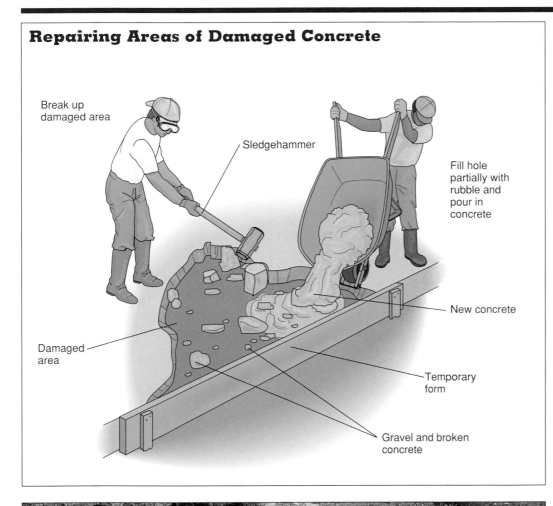

Break up damaged area

Sledgehammer

Fill hole partially with rubble and pour in concrete

New concrete

Damaged area

Temporary form

Gravel and broken concrete

bonding agent or grout dries, pack the patching compound into the hole. Trowel smooth, feathering the patch into the existing surface, and cure.

•Mending small cracks. If the crack is less than ⅛ inch wide, blow out any loose material and concrete dust. Apply the bonding agent or grout. Before it dries, fill the crack with a commercial patching compound, commercial cement-based grout, or a dry-pack mortar (see above). Trowel smooth, feathering the patch into the existing surface, and cure.

•Mending large cracks. For large cracks measuring more than ⅛ inch wide, use a hammer and cold chisel to clean out the crack and remove any loose or deteriorated concrete. Make the crack at least ¾ inch deep and undercut its sides so the patch can lock in place. Blow the loose material and concrete dust out of the cracks. Apply the bonding agent or grout. Before it dries, fill the crack with a dry-pack mortar (see above). Trowel smooth, feathering the patch into the existing concrete, and cure.

•Repairing severely cracked or damaged slabs. Decide whether the slab should be demolished or the damaged section rebuilt. Rebuild only if the damage doesn't extend over the entire slab. If you decide to rebuild, prepare to give the entire slab a 1-inch-thick topcoat of fresh concrete. Break up the damaged area with a jackhammer or sledgehammer and cold chisel (you can use the pieces as filler for the repair and to lift the slab if necessary). Roughen the undamaged

These chunks of broken concrete, together with new concrete castings and some creeping thyme, were transformed into a new patio.

areas of the slab for the new topcoat. Build temporary forms to accommodate the new height. Wet down the slab and wait until the standing water is absorbed. Make the concrete by mixing water with 1 part portland cement, 3 parts sand, and 3 parts aggregate in a batch sufficient to fill the damaged area and topcoat the entire slab. Apply a latex bonding agent over the slab. Before it dries, spread the concrete over the surface, and float. Finish and cure the same as for a slab (pages 80 and 81).

•Removing deteriorated divider boards. This less-than-desirable situation leaves you with no choice but to chisel the rotting wood out of the concrete. If it is anchored into the slab with nails, cut through them with a circular saw fitted with a diamond-edged blade. Clean out the joints thoroughly and trowel mortar into the gaps that remain. Let the mortar set up for two hours, then cut expansion joints in the fill strips with a grooving trowel or circular saw.

•Lifting a sunken slab. A slab that has settled can be raised to its original level by pumping flowable concrete under the sunken area. The concrete fills voids in the base and stabilizes the slab when it hardens. Called "slabjacking," this should be done by a contractor.

Extending a Concrete Patio

Enlarge an existing concrete patio simply by building a new concrete patio around or adjacent to it. Don't worry about the existing base crumbling when exposed; if it was

Resurfacing Concrete With a New Topcoat

Roughen Old Slab

Jackhammer

Spade bit

Scrub and Soak Slab

Float New Concrete

Screed

Temporary form

New layer of concrete, 1" thick

compacted correctly, it will stay intact. If some gravel escapes, push it back into place when you lay the new base.

After you've dug and filled the base, build the formwork, but do not attach it to the exposed sides of the existing slab. Instead, line these sides with flexible concrete joint foam. Drill 6-inch-deep horizontal holes through the foam and into the slab, placing them 2 to 3 feet apart at midheight on the sides of the slab. Cement 12-inch-long reinforcing rods into the holes. The 6 inches of rod projecting into the new slab area ties the new slab to the old, so they move together. Tie welded reinforcing mesh, held above the gravel with small stones or bits of brick or concrete, to the rods. Pour and finish the new slab, following the instructions for a concrete-slab patio beginning on page 75. The joint foam forms the expansion joint between the new and old slabs. The foam itself virtually disappears when the concrete is poured.

INDEX

U.S./Metric Measure Conversion Chart

		Formulas for Exact Measures			Rounded Measures for Quick Reference		
	Symbol	When you know:	Multiply by:	To find:			
Mass	oz	ounces	28.35	grams	1 oz		= 30 g
(weight)	lb	pounds	0.45	kilograms	4 oz		= 115 g
	g	grams	0.035	ounces	8 oz		= 225 g
	kg	kilograms	2.2	pounds	16 oz	= 1 lb	= 450 g
					32 oz	= 2 lb	= 900 g
					36 oz	= 2¼ lb	= 1000 g (1 kg)
Volume	pt	pints	0.47	liters	1 c	= 8 oz	= 250 ml
	qt	quarts	0.95	liters	2 c (1 pt)	= 16 oz	= 500 ml
	gal	gallons	3.785	liters	4 c (1 qt)	= 32 oz	= 1 liter
	ml	milliliters	0.034	fluid ounces	4 qt (1 gal)	= 128 oz	= 3¾ liter
Length	in.	inches	2.54	centimeters	⅜ in.	= 1.0 cm	
	ft	feet	30.48	centimeters	1 in.	= 2.5 cm	
	yd	yards	0.9144	meters	2 in.	= 5.0 cm	
	mi	miles	1.609	kilometers	2½ in.	= 6.5 cm	
	km	kilometers	0.621	miles	12 in. (1 ft)	= 30.0 cm	
	m	meters	1.094	yards	1 yd	= 90.0 cm	
	cm	centimeters	0.39	inches	100 ft	= 30.0 m	
					1 mi	= 1.6 km	
Temperature	°F	Fahrenheit	⅝ (after subtracting 32)	Celsius	32° F	= 0° C	
	°C	Celsius	⅘ (then add 32)	Fahrenheit	68° F	= 20° C	
					212° F	= 100° C	
Area	in.²	square inches	6.452	square centimeters	1 in.²	= 6.5 cm²	
	ft²	square feet	929.0	square centimeters	1 ft²	= 930.0 cm²	
	yd²	square yards	8361.0	square centimeters	1 yd²	= 8360.0 cm²	
	a.	acres	0.4047	hectares	1 a.	= 4050.0 m²	